AMAZING
Treasures

100+ Objects and Places That Will Boggle Your Mind

Written by **DAVID LONG**

Illustrations by **MUTI**

What on Earth Books

CONTENTS

Tikal, Guatemala

WHAT MAKES A TREASURE?

A treasure can be anything that's important or valuable to someone. Stories of pirates burying gold and jewels on a desert island are perhaps the most thrilling, but treasure can also include ancient artifacts—objects made by humans—that tell us about how people used to live, things people collect just for fun, or even the wonders of nature, which look so beautiful and play a vital part in keeping the planet healthy for all of us. Here are some examples of very different types of treasures.

Personal treasures

All treasures are special to someone. Some can be particularly rare or valuable, but they don't have to be jewels or ancient objects. A treasure can be as simple as a photograph or a favorite book. Is there something special that you treasure?

MASK OF AGAMEMNON

Greece

In 1876 a German archeologist named Heinrich Schliemann dug up a fabulous mask made of gold. This ancient artifact was more than 3,500 years old. It's one of five masks discovered in a series of royal graves at Mycenae, a historic site lying to the southwest of Athens, Greece's capital city. Schliemann borrowed the name Agamemnon from a king in Greek mythology, but we still don't know whose face is really shown on the mask or whose grave it came from.

Ancient civilizations

Long ago, people buried powerful rulers with precious objects, reflecting their status and power. At Mycenae, archeologists have discovered huge stores of gold, jewelry, and weapons in tombs.

TULIP BULBS
The Netherlands

In the early 1600s, rich collectors in the Netherlands became obsessed with the simple tulip. They especially wanted flowers in rare colors, and sometimes a single bulb sold for more than the price of a large house in the capital city. Prices climbed higher and higher, and then, in February 1637, they suddenly crashed. Almost overnight people had realized that a flower is only a flower, no matter what color it is. Many people instantly lost a fortune. A few may even have lost their homes when their businesses collapsed.

Exotic flowers

The tulip craze started when traders brought the flowers from Turkey to the Netherlands. Dutch scientists and painters, in particular, were fascinated by these new flowers. Like many treasures, they were highly valued because they seemed exotic and unusual.

ARCTIC SEA ICE
Arctic ocean

There's no land under the North Pole, just billions of tons of ice. It may not sound like treasure, but this ice is important to life on Earth—including ours—and this makes it something to treasure. Sea ice in the Arctic and the Antarctic keeps the polar regions cool. This helps to moderate the climate all around the world, including where you live. The vast expanses of ice reflect about 80 percent of the sunlight that strikes them back into space. If the ice melts and less sunlight is reflected back into space, global warming will continue to worsen, and the results could be catastrophic for everyone.

Land of the bears

The name "Arctic" comes from the word for "bear" in Latin, the language of the Romans. This far northern part of the Earth was named after a far north constellation of stars called the "Great Bear."

The Arctic ice has its own bears too: polar bears! Unfortunately, these bears are threatened by the shrinking of the ice sheets that they call home.

WHERE ARE TREASURES FOUND?

Treasures are found all over the world! Treasure can be buried or locked up to keep it safe, lost during wars or natural disasters, accidentally destroyed, or hidden away by secretive owners. Happily, today a lot of it is on display in museums where anyone can see it.

amphora (container with a slim neck and two handles)

Right beneath your feet

Treasures can turn up in unexpected places. Societies have come and gone in the past, and new people have moved into the same areas. Sometimes, when the new people build cities and homes, they bury a past society's treasures below them. There could be treasure beneath your feet right now!

rhyton (conical jug)

PANAGYURISHTE TREASURE
Bulgaria

Seven cups, a jug, and a bowl of pure 24-carat gold make up one of Bulgaria's most precious discoveries. Correctly known as seven rhytons, an amphora, and a phiale, they were made about 2,300 years ago. Archeologists think that they belonged to King Seuthes III. For more than 30 years, he was ruler of Thrace, a vanished Eastern European kingdom (Bulgaria is in the region where Thrace once was). Long ago somebody had buried the gold items, possibly to hide them from an invading army. But in 1949 three Bulgarian brothers dug them up outside a tile factory.

phiale (disk)

GREAT LIBRARY OF ALEXANDRIA
Egypt

From around 300 to 30 BCE, Egypt was ruled by pharaohs from powerful Greek dynasties. These rulers wanted to gather together all human knowledge in a single library, which would be the greatest in the ancient world. The information was stored on more than 400,000 rolls of papyrus, an early form of paper made from reeds. The pharaohs employed at least 100 scholars to write even more, until tragically the library was entirely destroyed, possibly by fire in 48 BCE.

Valuable knowledge

Knowledge helps us to solve problems and come up with new ideas. But in ancient times, without computers or printed books, storing knowledge was particularly difficult. That's one reason why ancient societies treasured books and other writing, and stored them in safe places such as huge libraries.

Lost to history

Nobody can be quite sure what the Great Library looked like or exactly where it was built. It's just one of many incredible treasures lost to history. But who knows—maybe one day it will be rediscovered.

SIR JOHN SOANE'S MUSEUM
UK

Museums are full of treasures, and sometimes a museum can be a treasure in itself. One museum today is made up of the house and collection of Sir John Soane, a collector and architect who lived in a maze-like home in London that was actually three huge houses joined together. He filled this house with thousands of pictures, sculptures, antiquities, and unique architectural fragments. These range from a 3,300-year-old Egyptian sarcophagus to examples of Soane's own imaginative designs. He gave the entire collection to the British government before his death in 1837, and a special law was passed by Parliament to ensure that nothing could be added to it, sold, or taken away. Today, it is free to visit.

plaster cast of the ancient Greek god Apollo

These heavy marble urns were used in ancient Roman funerals to hold the ashes of the deceased. They are decorated with characters and stories, including the story of Hercules.

Unusual collections
From ancient ruins to stamp collections, museums come in many surprising forms and are a great way to see treasures.

Museo Subacuático de Arte
Mexico
You'll need a scuba suit to visit this underwater collection of sculptures.

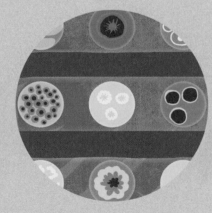

Micropia
The Netherlands
Microbes (microscopic organisms) are everywhere, and this museum is devoted exclusively to them.

Zigong Museum
China
Dinosaur museums contain fossil treasures. At Zigong museum, visitors can even visit a working dig site.

Origami Museum
Japan
The art of folding paper takes center stage in this collection.

WHO OWNS TREASURES?

Over the centuries, many treasures have been looted or stolen. It's hard to say who owns a treasure when the original owners are dead. Maybe we all do. Even if treasures end up in a museum where everyone can see them, it can be tricky to decide which museum and which country should have them, and people often disagree.

What's yours is mine

Pirates used to attack ships and take the treasures on board for themselves. Some would also take the crew and passengers as slaves. In a time when slavery was common, people themselves were treated like objects to be bought and sold. Of course, now we understand that each person owns herself or himself.

BENIN BRONZES

Nigeria

Around 1,000 beautiful bronze plaques were created to adorn a royal palace in what is now Nigeria. Produced about 500 years ago, they are outstanding examples of West African art. But today, very few of them are still in Africa. Most are displayed in European museums, rather than in Nigeria. The greatest number are in the British Museum in London. British soldiers took them there when much of this region of Africa was part of the British Empire.

Royal treasures

The bronzes depict the inhabitants of the Kingdom of Benin, which existed from the 1200s to the 1800s. They include images of the Oba (king), as well as soldiers and court officials. Some also show Europeans, who would ultimately loot the bronzes years later.

SVALBARD GLOBAL SEED VAULT

Norway

Imagine almost a million frozen seeds hidden inside a mountain near the North Pole. The Svalbard Global Seed Vault contains examples of the seeds of wheat, rice, maize, peas, beans, and other important food crops from around the world. There's room for 4.5 million species and up to 2.5 billion individual seeds. These are stored at 0°F (-18°C) and could be used to regrow any species wiped out by disease, climate change, or even nuclear war.

CORNELIUS GURLITT'S STOLEN HOARD

Germany

In 2012 German officials raided the apartment of a man named Cornelius Gurlitt, who was accused of not paying his taxes. Inside they found hundreds of paintings that had been stolen from Jews and other victims of the Nazis during World War II. The huge collection included priceless works by many of the most famous European artists. But it was no longer possible to trace the owners of all of the paintings, especially because many of them had been murdered during the war. So, the collection was put on display at a museum in Switzerland. The museum has agreed that any surviving children or grandchildren of the owners can reclaim the paintings or be paid for them, if they can prove that one of their ancestors owned them.

NATURAL WONDERS

Some of the most magnificent treasures aren't human-made, but come from the natural world. These are beautiful and extraordinary places, and their survival is important for all of us—and for the planet. Something that has taken millions of years to form or grow can't be replaced when it's gone. Also, if we damage our planet too much, we'll have nowhere else to live. Here are three natural wonders that we need to protect.

Rain forests, such as the Amazon, are made up of layers:

At the top is the emergent layer, where a few very tall trees stick out. These are home to large birds such as eagles and vultures.

Next is the canopy, which forms the leafy "roof" of the rainforest. Many animals live here, including monkeys and sloths.

Harpy eagle

Black howler monkey

Vampire bat

Toucan

AMAZON RAIN FOREST
South America

Spanning nine different countries, the world's largest forest covers over 2 million square miles (5.5 million square km). That's eight times the size of Texas. It's home to an incredible 1,300 bird species, 3,000 types of fish, hundreds of different mammals, and an enormous 2.5 million different insects. There are also more trees here than anywhere on the planet—as many as 390 billion of them. These make lots of oxygen, which we breathe, and soak up some of the gases that are dangerously warming our planet. Scientists estimate that this leafy green landscape makes about 6 to 9 percent of all the oxygen produced in the world.

Below the canopy is the understory. Smaller animals such as frogs and bats live in this damp, shaded layer.

Jaguar

At the bottom is the forest floor, which swarms with insects, centipedes, and spiders. Large mammals are on the prowl too, including anteaters and jaguars.

Anaconda

Deforestation
The Amazon rain forest is under threat from logging. Trees are cut down to clear space for growing crops or raising livestock. The wood is used for building or made into furniture.

Leatherback turtle

Leopard shark

GREAT BARRIER REEF
Australia

The world's largest coral reef lies off the coast of Queensland, Australia, and is more than 1,600 miles (2,600 km) from end to end. Parts of it are half a million years old, and the whole thing was made by vast numbers of tiny creatures called polyps. These produce the limestone shapes we call coral, which are home to hundreds of thousands of colorful fish and ferocious sharks. The polyps themselves are usually no larger than a pinhead, but over thousands of years, they have built a reef that is so massive it can be seen from space.

Don't touch!

Coral comes in lots of beautiful shapes and colors, but it is fragile. Even touching the coral can seriously damage it. To protect the reef, the Australian government has made taking coral home illegal in most cases.

Clownfish

MAMMOTH CAVE
USA

Mammoth Cave is the perfect name for the world's longest cave system. It's around ten million years old and stretches for more than 400 miles (640 km) beneath the ground in Kentucky. That's at least twice the length of its closest rival, an underwater cave in Mexico. No one has ever explored the whole of it. In fact, it's so long that visitors on even the longest tours, which take around six hours, will only ever see a tiny fraction of this natural wonder.

Ancient rocks

The amazing rock formations in Mammoth Cave have formed over millions of years. Stalactites hang from the ceiling, and stalagmites rise up from the ground. The most unusual of all are "gypsum flowers"—twisting crystal formations that look like flowers.

— Stalactite

Stalagmite

INCREDIBLE ARTWORKS

Humans have been creating art for tens of thousands of years and for many different reasons. The best art is breathtakingly beautiful or intriguing. Sometimes ancient art might have been for decoration, but often it was connected to cultural rituals and religious ceremonies, or provided a way to send information from one community to another. It can tell us a lot about the way our ancestors lived their lives.

ABORIGINAL ROCK ART
Australia

Some of the oldest art in the world was created by indigenous Australian people. Aboriginal peoples settled in Australia at least 60,000 years ago, long, long before the first Europeans arrived in the 1600s. Their varied artistic creations include rock carvings, ground designs, and body painting. The most ancient examples are thought to date back at least 40,000 years. They may have been produced as a way of sharing and communicating stories, details of everyday lives, and important religious rituals across generations at a time before there was a written language.

LASCAUX CAVE PAINTINGS
France

In 1940 a series of colorful paintings was discovered by four teenage boys and a dog named Robot while they were exploring some caves in southwestern France. The elaborate images were made during the Stone Age, up to 20,000 years ago. They include wild animals, strange symbols, and only occasionally human figures. More than 2,000 images have been found so far, many painted with colors made from burnt wood, bones, or river clay and mud. Unfortunately these materials are so fragile that even a person's breath can damage them. To keep the art safe, the caves are no longer open to the public.

LÖWENMENSCH
Germany

Known as Lion Man, this carving is more than 40,000 years old and was found in a German cave in 1939. It is the oldest known example of art that depicts the figure of a living creature. The figure has both human and animal features, making this a kind of art called "zoomorphism." It was carved out of a mammoth tusk. Although it is only slightly more than a foot (30 cm) tall, it would have taken many hours to carve using simple stone tools. Life in the prehistoric world was harsh and dangerous. The Lion Man shows us that, even in these conditions, our ancestors still thought it was important to create beautiful artistic or religious objects.

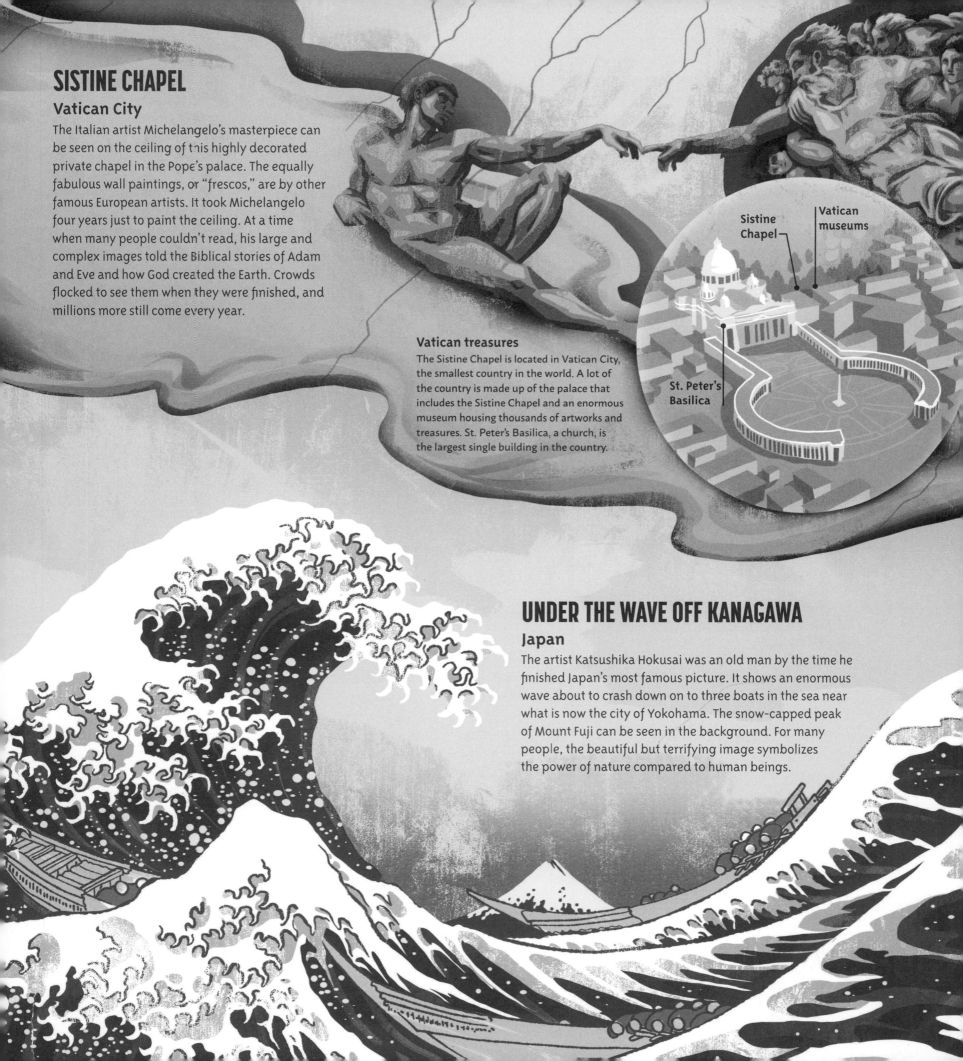

SISTINE CHAPEL
Vatican City

The Italian artist Michelangelo's masterpiece can be seen on the ceiling of this highly decorated private chapel in the Pope's palace. The equally fabulous wall paintings, or "frescos," are by other famous European artists. It took Michelangelo four years just to paint the ceiling. At a time when many people couldn't read, his large and complex images told the Biblical stories of Adam and Eve and how God created the Earth. Crowds flocked to see them when they were finished, and millions more still come every year.

Vatican treasures

The Sistine Chapel is located in Vatican City, the smallest country in the world. A lot of the country is made up of the palace that includes the Sistine Chapel and an enormous museum housing thousands of artworks and treasures. St. Peter's Basilica, a church, is the largest single building in the country.

Sistine Chapel

Vatican museums

St. Peter's Basilica

UNDER THE WAVE OFF KANAGAWA
Japan

The artist Katsushika Hokusai was an old man by the time he finished Japan's most famous picture. It shows an enormous wave about to crash down on to three boats in the sea near what is now the city of Yokohama. The snow-capped peak of Mount Fuji can be seen in the background. For many people, the beautiful but terrifying image symbolizes the power of nature compared to human beings.

TREASURED RUINS

Some of the most magnificent buildings in the world now lie in ruins. For thousands of years, even the richest and most advanced civilizations built ordinary homes out of mud or wood. These have hardly ever survived. Only the most important buildings were made from stone, so temples, royal tombs, and fortresses are often all that's left. We can still tell a lot by looking at these ruins. Wandering through them, it is easy to imagine what life must have been like for the people who built them or lived in them.

PARTHENON
Greece

This gleaming marble temple is the most eye-catching building in Athens, Greece's capital city. It sits high up on a rocky hill called the Acropolis. The temple was once dedicated to Athena, the ancient Greek goddess of wisdom. Many of its finest features have since been taken away and are on display in museums in Britain, France, and Denmark. Even so, the beautiful 2,500-year-old ruin still dominates the modern city. In the 1600s, it was occupied by a Turkish army and badly damaged in an explosion. Today, the greatest threat to its stonework is pollution from cars down in the streets below.

Athena, ancient Greek goddess of wisdom

GREAT PYRAMID AND GREAT SPHINX
Egypt

The Great Pyramid of Giza was the world's tallest man-made structure for an incredible 3,800 years. Even today, the pyramid towers over the Egyptian countryside. More than 450 feet (140 m) tall, it was built as a tomb for a powerful pharaoh, Khufu, who died in 2566 BCE. Nearby is a mysterious 240-foot (73-m-) long statue of a mythical creature called a Sphinx. It has the body of a lion and a huge human head, but no one knows who built it or why.

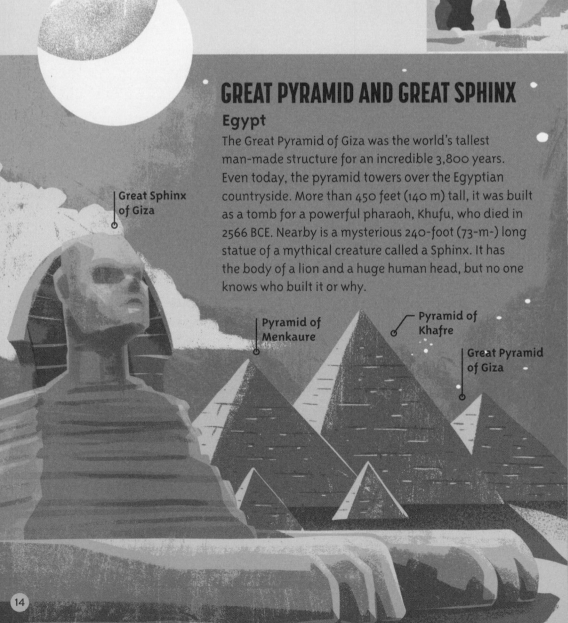

Great Sphinx of Giza

Pyramid of Menkaure

Pyramid of Khafre

Great Pyramid of Giza

MASADA
Israel

After the Romans invaded the region of modern-day Israel and Palestine nearly 2,000 years ago, many of the Jews living there took shelter in this mountaintop fortress overlooking the Dead Sea. They defended themselves for as long as they could, but they knew that they were almost certain to lose against the powerful Roman army. The Jews decided to kill themselves rather than be captured and enslaved. Because of this sacrifice, Masada has become a symbol of courage, determination, and personal freedom.

MACHU PICCHU
Peru

An abandoned city situated 7,900 feet (2,400 m) up in the Andes mountains, Machu Picchu was built high on some cliffs for the Inca king Pachacuti. Incas were skilled builders, and their buildings were made to survive earthquakes. They carried all the stone for construction on foot or using llamas. The Inca Empire, however, was eventually destroyed by Spanish invaders who came looking for gold. Centuries later, despite their remote location, these picturesque ruins are one of South America's most visited sites.

KNOSSOS PALACE
Greece

Knossos is often described as Europe's oldest city. Its large palace lay at the center of the important Bronze Age Minoan civilization. The Minoans flourished on the large island of Crete from 2000 to around 1450 BCE. The Minoans who lived at Knossos were highly sophisticated people. Many could read and write, and their buildings were up to four stories high. These had ventilation systems and even plumbing hundreds of years before the Greeks and Romans.

PALMYRA
Syria

This ruined city in the scorching Syrian Desert was once a hub for rich merchants trading between Europe and Asia. Invaded and looted by the Roman army about 1,700 years ago, it slowly became less important to traders until it was mostly abandoned. The temples, tall columns, and elaborate monuments left behind have attracted many people interested in archeology and architecture. Sadly the ruins have been badly damaged in the Syrian civil war, which began in 2011. Many of the city's treasures were deliberately smashed or stolen by rebel soldiers.

RICH ROYALS

For most of history, emperors, kings, and queens were nearly always the richest, most powerful people in their own countries. Some of the most amazing treasures were created for them. These could range from tiny jewels to vast palaces, and even the smallest of them could be worth many times what an ordinary person could expect to earn in a year—or even a lifetime.

JACOB DIAMOND
India

This enormous gemstone is said to be the fifth largest diamond in the world. It was once owned by the fabulously wealthy Nizam, or ruler, of Hyderabad, an area of central India. The last Nizam found the gem in a shoe in his palace. It had been left there to be forgotten by his father, who was angry about a dispute that happened when he was buying it. Despite its value, the last Nizam used it as a paperweight to keep the things on his desk in order. Today it is kept in a vault and owned by the Indian government, along with most of the Nizam's other jewels.

BUST OF NEFERTITI
Egypt

One of the most powerful women in ancient Egypt, Queen Nefertiti was the wife of Pharaoh Akhenaten. Thousands of years after she was queen, Nefertiti was made famous again by the discovery, in 1912, of this striking painted sculpture. It shows a beautiful woman with strong features and a long, elegant neck. The sculpture has become one of the most copied pieces of art from ancient times. Nefertiti and Akhenaten wanted ordinary Egyptians to worship a single sun god named "Aten," but after their deaths, people went back to worshipping lots of other gods and goddesses.

FABERGÉ EGGS
Russia

Peter Carl Fabergé was the greatest jeweler of the late 1800s and early 1900s. His most famous creations were these elaborate enameled Easter eggs. He made them for the Russian tsars, or emperors, Alexander III and Nicholas II. Each one contained a different "surprise." One egg included a miniature gold clockwork train, while another opened to reveal a tiny mechanical peacock. Only about forty-six have survived, and several now belong to Queen Elizabeth II of the UK. A single one of these eggs can sell for millions of dollars.

Royal celebration
Several of the eggs were made to commemorate special events, such as the coronation of an empress or the completion of the railway from European Russia to the far east of Siberia.

WINDSOR CASTLE

UK

The largest continually inhabited castle in the world is also one of the very oldest. It was built nearly 1,000 years ago, just after the Norman Conquest of England in 1066. It's been a royal residence for almost as long as that. The medieval King Edward III was born within its thick stone walls. King Henry VIII came to Windsor to hunt, play tennis, and write songs. And Prince Albert, husband to queen Victoria, died in one of its rooms. Even now the Queen of the UK, Elizabeth II, spends most of her weekends here at her favorite castle. When a part of it caught fire in 1992, nearly two million gallons (7 million liters) of water were needed to save this precious medieval survivor.

Upper Ward

The eastern courtyard, called the Upper Ward, contains apartments and rooms for royalty and visitors. The rooms are decorated in many lavish styles.

The Round Tower

This tall building is built on the site of the original castle, constructed by the Normans in the 1100s.

Unusual treasures

The royal collection of treasures at Windsor Castle includes many priceless objects, but the most unique may be a dollhouse. The tiny house is complete with working faucets and a flushable toilet, a library stocked with real, miniature books, and a hidden garden that can be pulled out from underneath like a drawer.

Lower Ward

The western courtyard, called the Lower Ward, includes the main chapel for the castle, as well as the Curfew Tower, which once contained a dungeon.

LOST TREASURES

Several of the world's greatest treasures haven't been seen for centuries. Some have been hidden away deliberately, stolen, or simply lost. A few have almost certainly been destroyed. But one day perhaps at least some of them will be rediscovered and put on display. Here are a few mysterious lost treasures to look out for.

LA NOCHE TRISTE TREASURE
Mexico

The Spanish invaders of Mexico called it "la noche triste" ("the night of sorrows") when the indigenous Aztecs fought and killed many of their comrades in 1520. During the battle, all the gold the Spaniards had stolen from the Aztecs vanished. For a long time, it was thought that it had been dropped into the deep waters of a nearby lake, but people have never found anything there. Mexico City was later built over the site of the battle, and a gold bar dug up during modern construction work was found to be part of the treasure. Even more gold could still be lying deep beneath the city's crowded streets waiting to be discovered.

AMBER ROOM
Russia

In the 1700s, the walls of this stunning chamber were covered from floor to ceiling in precious amber, a type of fossilized tree sap. The room was originally built as an expensive gift from the king of Prussia (now an area of northern Poland) to the Russian tsar, or emperor. When it was completed, it must have looked spectacular. Unfortunately, about 200 years later, it was taken apart and the glittering golden-red panels were carried away by the German army. No one has seen them since World War II ended in 1945.

KING JOHN'S JEWELS
UK

John was an unpopular English king during the 1200s. He had many enemies but still managed to reign for seventeen years. While fighting to stay in power, he is thought to have lost his crown jewels in thick mud as he traveled across a marsh in England. He died shortly afterwards. Now, more than 800 years later, treasure hunters with metal detectors are still trying to figure out exactly where the jewels were lost.

WALBRZYCH GOLD TRAIN
Poland

During World War II, Nazi Germany stole hundreds of tons of gold, jewels, and other treasures from the countries they conquered and the people they killed. This stolen loot was carried back to Germany in trucks and trains by military units called the Kunstschutz. Most of it got there, but some treasure hunters think that one train disappeared along the way. They think it was driven into a secret network of tunnels beneath Poland's Owl Mountains. These giant tunnels definitely exist (they were dug out by the Germans' prisoners, who were treated like slaves), but so far no one has found the train full of treasure.

MANSA MUSA'S TREASURE
Mali

During the 1300s, Musa was the mansa, or emperor, of Mali in West Africa, and one of the richest men who ever lived. Most of his wealth came from slavery and gold mining. The emperors of Mali were all devout Muslims who made the hajj, or religious pilgrimage, to the holy city of Mecca. On his pilgrimage, Mansa Musa gave away so much gold to the people he met on his way to Mecca that it damaged the economies of the countries he visited. However, when he died, his heirs were not able to hold on to his wealth. Now Mansa Musa's treasure is scattered, and no one knows for sure how many billions of dollars it might have been worth.

OAK ISLAND TREASURE
Canada

Since the late 1700s, stories of a lost treasure on Oak Island have gone from local legend to international mystery. According to different accounts, the treasure could be a pirate's hoard, a French queen's jewels, top-secret documents, or even the Holy Grail, a legendary Christian relic. No one actually knows what the Oak Island treasure is or where it is buried. Even so, explorers, including two famous Hollywood actors and even an American president, have spent a fortune looking for it. For more than 200 years, people have combed this tiny island searching for clues, but so far no one has found even the tiniest bit of treasure. Perhaps the real mystery is why they keep looking...

MYSTERIOUS TREASURES

Sometimes archeologists and explorers find things they can't understand. Ancient writing can take decades or even centuries to decode. A piece of machinery can be impossible to operate if a part of it has broken off and gotten lost. Even a statue can be confusing to someone who doesn't understand the civilization that created it.

Studying the sky
The Antikythera Mechanism may have helped early scientists to predict solar eclipses, which were important events in many ancient civilizations.

ANTIKYTHERA MECHANISM

Greece

The strangely named Antikythera mechanism could be a rusty remnant of the world's first computer. Discovered on a shipwreck at the start of the 1900s, this ingenious clockwork device is more than 2,000 years old. It is thought to have used thirty-seven individual bronze wheels to calculate the movements of the Moon and the Sun. Sadly it doesn't work after so long underwater, but it has become one of the most popular exhibits at the National Archeological Museum in Athens.

MOAI HEADS

Easter Island (Chile)

Around 1,000 giant stone heads are the most visible reminders of the Rapa Nui people, who lived on Easter Island in the Pacific Ocean from as early as 400 CE onward. The heads—called moai—were probably produced to honor the Rapa Nui's ancestors, but nothing was written down to confirm this. They weigh up to 200 tons (180 tonnes) each, so they must have required hundreds of people to carve and move them into place. They show that this was once an advanced civilization that mostly disappeared. Some people think the Rapa Nui chopped down so many trees to make way for farming that their island eventually became mostly uninhabitable and populations collapsed.

PHAISTOS DISK

Greece

In 1908 an archeologist found a disk of fired or hardened clay while excavating a palace in Phaistos, on the island of Crete. It is decorated on both sides with dozens of strange symbols. To this day, no one has managed to explain what these mean. Some experts think they may spell out a prayer; others suggest the disc is a sort of early calendar. Most agree, however, that the disc's secret code probably won't be cracked unless other, similar discs can be found elsewhere on the island.

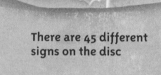

Palace culture

The Phaistos disc was discovered at Phaistos, one of the cities of the ancient Minoan civilization. This culture flourished on Crete, in Greece, from 2000 to 1450 BCE. Minoan rulers lived in grand palaces, the largest of which was at Knossos.

There are 45 different signs on the disc

Turning the disc over reveals more writing

Mystery scripts

After lots of study, historians can learn to read many texts from ancient cultures or civilizations that have vanished, but some remain a mystery. Here are a few that are still waiting to be deciphered:

Rongorongo

Like the moai heads, this script from Easter Island shows that an advanced society once lived on the island. The script is written using pictures and symbols. Some of them look like animals or plants from Easter Island.

Indus Valley

The Indus Valley civilization that used this script existed for 2,000 years along the Indus river between India and Pakistan. Some of the world's oldest cities were built by this civilization, which developed around 3500 BCE.

Zapotec

The ancient civilizations of Mesoamerica, such as the Aztec, Maya, and Zapotec, built large cities and had various systems for writing, counting, and keeping track of the days. Zapotec writing may be the oldest, but it is also the most poorly understood.

HISTORY AND LEGENDS

Stories have always been important, but they don't have to be written down to be remembered. In fact, for much of human history, most ordinary people couldn't read or write. Some cultures have passed their stories from one generation to the next just by talking to each other and listening. Others have created paintings or tapestries, performed plays, or recited epic poems to explain often quite detailed events. These are some of the most valuable stories ever told.

EPIC OF GILGAMESH
Iraq

This story is believed to be the oldest ever written down. It is at least 3,400 years old and describes the adventures of a legendary king called Gilgamesh. He ruled the city of Uruk, which was located in what is now Iraq. His story is told as a long poem using writing symbols called "cuneiform." These wedge-shaped marks were pressed into wet clay tablets, which were then baked hard in the sun. Experts think there may be some parts of the story missing. The epic poem is so long that it was split over twelve tablets, and it would take most readers about two hours to finish it.

BAYEUX TAPESTRY
France

This 230-foot- (70-m-) long piece of embroidery was created to celebrate the successful invasion of England by William the Conqueror. William was ruler of the Normans from northern France and defeated King Harold of England. It tells the story from the winners' point of view, and was made in England shortly after the Battle of Hastings in 1066, when King Harold was defeated. Stitched in many different colors on a strip of woven linen, it looks like an old-fashioned cartoon. Actually, it is an incredibly detailed historical account.

Death of a king
One of the most gruesome scenes shows Harold with an arrow stuck in his eye.

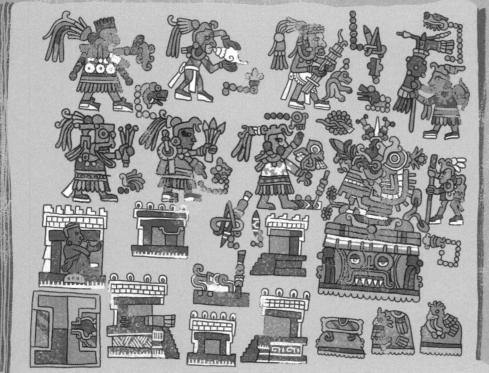

CODEX ZOUCHE-NUTTALL
Mexico

The Codex is a document from the 1300s to 1400s, painted on an 36-foot- (11-m-) long strip of deerskin. It's kept by the British Museum and is enormously rare. Fewer than twenty documents survive from this period in what is now Mexico. The Codex shows the military conquests and alliances of several different rulers of a small kingdom. Using pictures rather than words, it describes how the greatest of them, Lord Eight Deer Jaguar Claw, conquered ninety-four cities. But he eventually got too greedy and was killed by his own family.

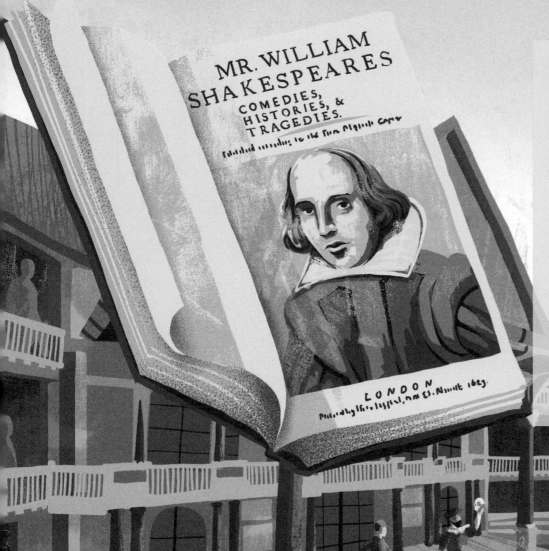

SHAKESPEARE'S FIRST FOLIO
UK

William Shakespeare completed almost forty plays and wrote more than 150 sonnets, a type of poem. He died around 400 years ago but is still regarded by many as the most important writer in the English language and the greatest playwright of all time.

Shakespeare's plays were enormously popular in the late 1500s and early 1600s in London, England, where he also worked as an actor. People loved watching his plays, which covered many different subjects, including love, hate, jealousy, revenge, grief, death, murder, magic, and mystery. They are still performed around the world today. His lasting popularity means that original copies of his plays are enormously valuable. The First Folio is the name given to a collection of his plays that was printed a few years after he died in 1616. At that time, a copy would have cost just 15 shillings (around $130 in today's money). In 2006, one of the rare survivors sold for over $3.6 million.

TREASURE HOARDS

Treasure can mean different things to different people. Even so, there will always be something special about discovering a cave, a hole in the ground, or even just an old broken pot stuffed with gold, silver, and precious jewels.

CHEAPSIDE HOARD
UK

In 1912 workmen stumbled upon a glittering hoard of around 500 gems and jewels lying in the soil beneath one of London's busiest streets. The treasures came from all over the world. They may have been buried to protect them during the English Civil War that took place from 1642 to 1646. The Cheapside Hoard is the world's largest single collection of jewelry from the late-1500s and 1600s in England, and has now become one of the most popular exhibits at the Museum of London in the UK.

BACTRIAN GOLD
Afghanistan

This incredible collection of nearly 21,000 items was discovered in 1978 in six burial mounds belonging to five women and a man. The coins, jewelry, ornaments, and other artifacts of gold, silver, and ivory are more than 2,000 years old. One fabulous Indian coin, decorated with a lion, is evidence of the trade that took place on the Silk Road, the trade route that connected Asia with Europe.

On the move

The people who buried the Bactrian gold in ancient times were probably nomads. This means they didn't have a permanent home but stayed on the move instead. One skeleton was found with a foldable crown. This could have been useful for packing it away somewhere safe when the group needed to move on.

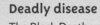

ERFURT AND COLMAR HOARDS
Germany and France

These important discoveries were found in two towns in Germany and France. They include cups, bowls, and medieval Jewish wedding rings. Many are made of gold, and they are thought to have been hidden underground to keep them safe during the period of the Black Death. This terrible epidemic swept across Europe and parts of Asia in the 1300s and killed between 75 and 200 million people.

Deadly disease

The Black Death was a type of disease called bubonic plague. Without the understanding of disease we have today, some people blamed other groups, such as Jews, for the plague. Doctors did exist, but they weren't very effective. These "plague doctors" were recognizable from their long coats and hooked masks.

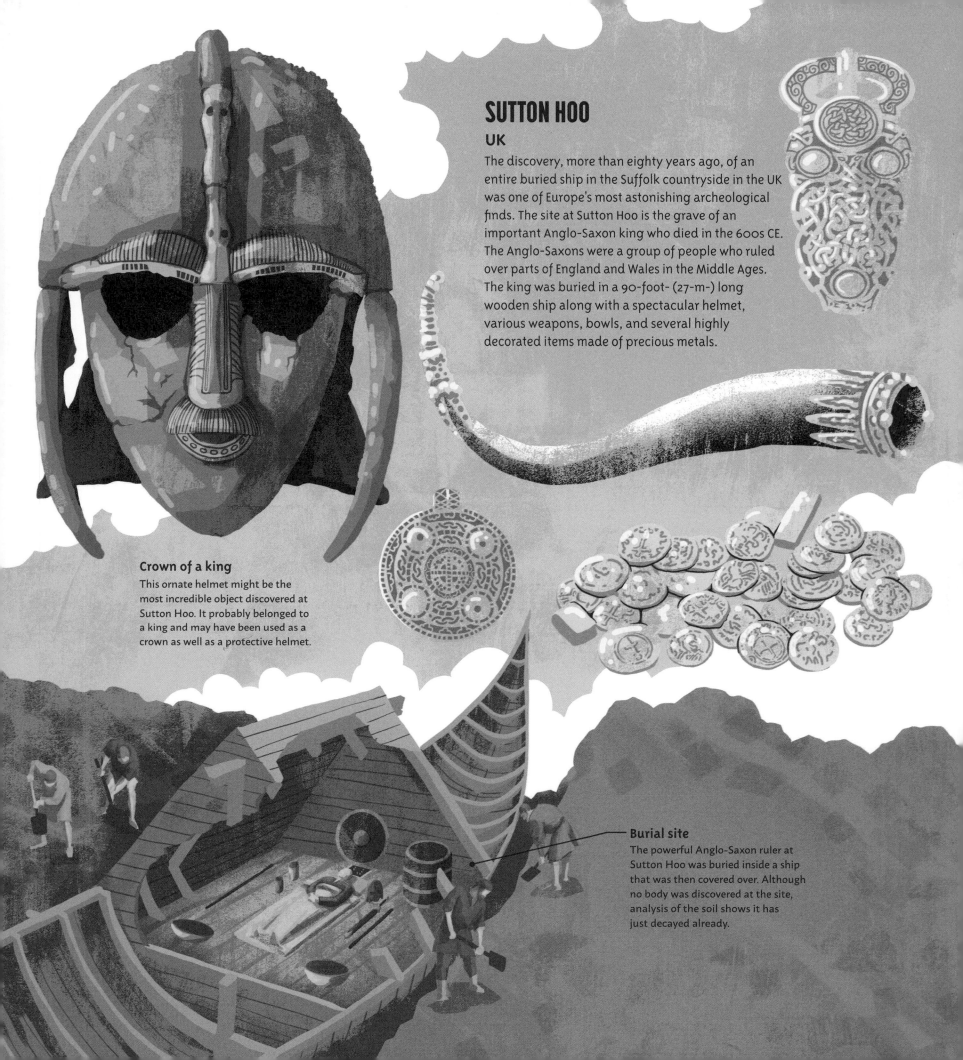

SUTTON HOO

UK

The discovery, more than eighty years ago, of an entire buried ship in the Suffolk countryside in the UK was one of Europe's most astonishing archeological finds. The site at Sutton Hoo is the grave of an important Anglo-Saxon king who died in the 600s CE. The Anglo-Saxons were a group of people who ruled over parts of England and Wales in the Middle Ages. The king was buried in a 90-foot- (27-m-) long wooden ship along with a spectacular helmet, various weapons, bowls, and several highly decorated items made of precious metals.

Crown of a king

This ornate helmet might be the most incredible object discovered at Sutton Hoo. It probably belonged to a king and may have been used as a crown as well as a protective helmet.

Burial site

The powerful Anglo-Saxon ruler at Sutton Hoo was buried inside a ship that was then covered over. Although no body was discovered at the site, analysis of the soil shows it has just decayed already.

TREASURE HOARDS
CONTINUED

FORT KNOX
USA

Hidden inside a secure building on a US army base is one of the largest collections of gold in the world. The location's real name is the United States Bullion Depository, but lots of people call it Fort Knox after the 170-square-mile (440-square-km) army base it's in. Its underground vaults have room for almost 5,000 tons (4,500 tonnes) of solid gold worth around $200 billion. Hundreds of specially trained police guards and up to 25,000 soldiers make sure that Fort Knox has never been broken into.

WONOBOYO HOARD
Indonesia

In 1990 farmworkers digging in a field on the slopes of a volcano called Mount Merapi on the island of Java discovered some old pots in the soil. They were more than 1,000 years old and contained 77 pounds (35 kg) of gleaming gold treasures. The finds included elaborate jewelry that may have belonged to an ancient king of Java. Also discovered were two bracelets made for elephants and religious objects thought to have come from a nearby Hindu temple.

HARALD BLUETOOTH HOARD
Germany

A 13-year-old boy helped to find a rare Viking silver coin on an island off the coast of Germany in 2018. When archeologists began exploring the site, they found silver jewelry, about 600 coins, and a decorative hammer. Hammers like this were associated with the Viking god of thunder, Thor. The treasures are thought to have belonged to Harald Bluetooth. This Danish king fled to Germany in the 900s after losing a battle against his own son.

Thor's Hammer pendant

LONDON SILVER VAULTS
UK

More than 100 years ago, a secure top-secret underground vault was built in London in the UK for wealthy people and, later, jewelers to store their most valuable items. Today it is a highly specialized market, with more than thirty shops selling the world's largest selection of new and antique silver. The walls are so thick that when an air raid in 1940 completely destroyed the building above, the vaults were left undamaged.

PRICELESS KNOWLEDGE

It is hard to appreciate the value of something written in a strange language you don't understand. However, to those who can read them, the knowledge contained in ancient scrolls and manuscripts can be more valuable than a pirate's plunder or the jewels of the richest queen.

GUTENBERG BIBLE
Germany

For centuries, most books had to be handwritten and were very expensive. Then, in the mid-1400s, Johannes Gutenberg invented a way of printing books far more easily and cheaply. Printing would change the world forever as more people than ever started to read. The Bible was one of the first books to be printed in Europe, but only about twenty complete copies of Gutenberg's original Bible still exist. This makes them very valuable. Most are now owned by universities, and they are said to be worth at least $26 million each.

COMPLETE LIBRARY OF THE FOUR TREASURES
China

Also known as the Siku Quanshu, this was the largest collection of books in Chinese history. It belonged to the Qianlong Emperor, who reigned from 1735 to 1796, and included a catalog of 10,680 different books put together by hundreds of scholars. The emperor ordered more than 3,800 scribes to copy out every word from about 3,500 of these books, which were collected from all over China, by hand. When they finished, they had written out a total of more than 2.3 million pages.

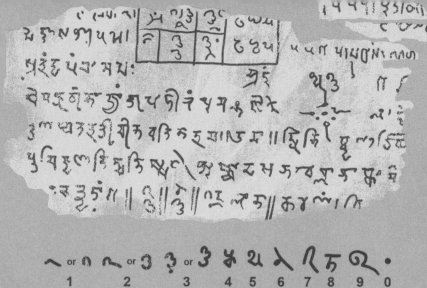

BAKHSHALI MANUSCRIPT
Pakistan

This is the earliest known example of Indian mathematics. It is at least 1,000 years old and written on seventy pieces of flattened bark from a birch tree. The real name of the author is unknown, but the scribe who wrote the manuscript is described as a "king of calculators."

New numbers

The symbols that we now use for numbers, such as "2" for the number two, were first developed in ancient India. Some symbols in the Bakhshali manuscript, such as 2 and 3, might look familiar. The author may also have been the first to use a symbol for zero—a simple dot.

VATICAN LIBRARY
Vatican City

One of the oldest, largest libraries in the world, the Vatican Library belongs to the Catholic Church. It was officially established in 1475, more than 500 years ago, and contains around two million books, documents, and manuscripts. These include the oldest complete copy of the Christian Bible (from the early 300s CE) as well as thousands of books from other religions. Researchers are allowed to use the library, but no more than 200 of them at a time.

DA MING HUN YI TU MAP
China

This is a large map, almost 13 feet (4 m) tall and 15 feet (4.5 m) wide, that shows China's Ming Empire lying at the center of the world. It was painted on silk in the late 1300s and is the oldest map ever found in this region. Detailed maps like this were vital for controlling such a large country, and for centuries, the map was kept in the Forbidden City, China's imperial palace complex. Now it forms part of the important First Historical Archive of China in Beijing.

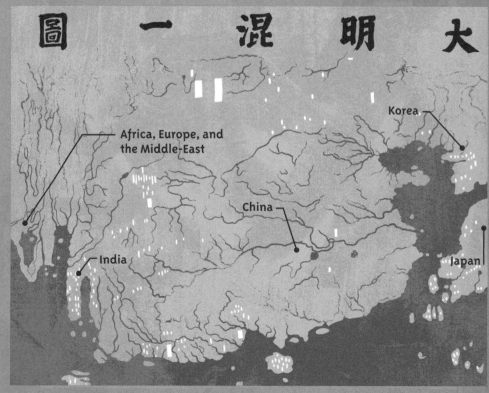

WORLD OF TREASURES

Treasures can be found all over the world: in museums or ancient ruins, or buried underground. They could be hiding in attics or sunk at the bottom of the ocean. Fold out the flaps for a map of all the treasures in this book, in the order they appear. As you can see, treasures have no boundaries. They can be found on every continent and in the ocean, too.

CAHOKIA MOUNDS
USA
These enormous mounds were built by people from the Mississippian culture. Constructed around 800 and 1350 CE, they formed part of an enormous city.

PERITO MORENO GLACIER
Argentina
Glaciers are enormous bodies of slow-moving ice. Some started to form tens of thousands of years ago. The Perito Moreno Glacier in Argentina is one of the largest in the world, covering an area of over 100 square miles (260 square km).

HERMITAGE
Russia
This ornate museum was started by Russian Empress Catherine the Great. The main parts of its collection are spread over six buildings. With more than 3 million items, the collection is one of the largest in the world.

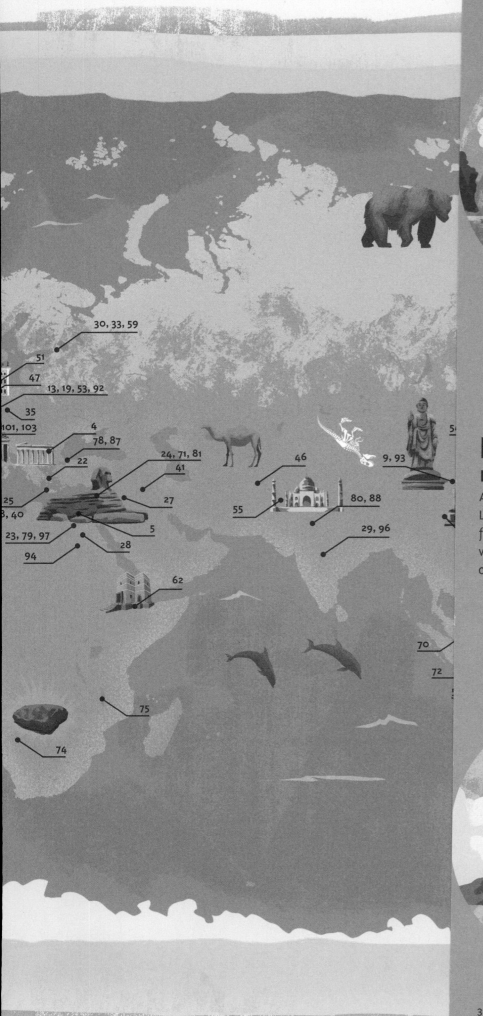

30, 33, 59

51

47

13, 19, 53, 92

35

101, 103

4

78, 87

22

24, 71, 81

41

46

9, 93

25

8, 40

27

55

80, 88

23, 79, 97

5

29, 96

94

28

62

70

72

75

74

RAI STONES
Micronesia

These carved stone discs on the Micronesian island of Yap in the Pacific Ocean may be the most unusual coins in the world. Islanders have used them as a currency for many centuries, although today they mainly use American dollars. They range from just about an inch (2.5 cm) in diameter to a whopping 12 feet (3.6 m).

LALIBELA
Ethiopia

A holy site in Ethiopia, Lalibela is most famous for its enormous churches, which are cut directly out of the surrounding rock.

ITSUKUSHIMA SHRINE
Japan

This island temple in Japan is famous for its O-Torii gate, a symbolic entrance to the shrine, which seems to float in the water when the tide is right.

THE FORBIDDEN CITY

China

Home to China's emperors for almost 500 years, Beijing's spectacular Forbidden City is a vast, rectangular complex of nearly 1,000 buildings. It was really a palace rather than a city and is still the largest ancient palace on Earth. covering an area of 0.5 square miles (1.2 square km). That's about the same as 111 soccer fields. Building it took a million workers an incredible fourteen years. Today it is also the largest collection of preserved wooden buildings anywhere in the world.

Dozens of elegant palaces, temples, and courtyards are surrounded by high defensive walls and a water-filled moat more than 160 feet (50 m) wide. The colorful architecture and rich decoration influenced building styles in this region for centuries, although nothing this grand was ever built again. Almost every building has a roof of glazed yellow tiles: yellow is traditionally associated with the Chinese emperors. At each of the city's four corners is a tall guard tower. Between these towers are four ceremonial gateways. The main gate, called the Meridian Gate or Wumen, is in the southern wall. It has five arches, and historically it was the most important entrance to the Forbidden City. It is also where officials who displeased the emperor were beaten as punishment for all to see.

Twenty-four different emperors lived in the Forbidden City from 1420 to 1912. Many of the buildings were occupied by the emperor's family and his staff, who spent much of their lives within its walls. Important government officials, who helped run the huge country of China, visited the palace every day. Hundreds of servants were also employed to look after more than 8,700 rooms and to clean the 1.6 million square feet (150,000 square m) of polished floor! There are no emperors or palace servants here now, however, because for most of the last century the complex has been a truly extraordinary museum.

The inner court areas included the splendid private palaces and gardens of the Imperial family.

The Meridian Gate was the largest of the four entrances to the Forbidden City.

The outer court areas contained government offices, temples, and palaces where the Emperor would meet important visitors.

The treasures inside the museum are mostly from the Ming and Qing dynasties. These were the final two Chinese dynasties, covering a period from the 1300s until 1912. Over seventeen million visitors a year come to see the collection, which includes about 50,000 paintings! The museum also has 350,000 pieces of china; 35,000 items of bronze, jade, and precious stones; and over 1,500 clocks, many of them antique. Most of the objects on display are Chinese, but not all of them. Several Chinese emperors acquired luxury items from overseas, from countries such as the UK, France, Switzerland, Japan, and the USA. Often visitors to Beijing presented these objects to the Chinese rulers as prestigious gifts.

SUNKEN TREASURES

Around the world, there are millions of shipwrecks lying on the seabed. Some were sunk in ferocious storms or in battle, others after hitting rocks or icebergs. They range from a few years old to a few thousand. While not all of them were carrying treasure, they have become treasures themselves and more than a few have given up their precious secrets.

1 RMS TITANIC
Atlantic Ocean

Probably the most famous ship of all time, the *Titanic* sank after hitting an iceberg in 1912. More than 1,500 passengers and crew died when the luxury liner plunged nearly 2.5 miles (4 km) to the bottom of the north Atlantic Ocean. Anything connected with the disaster is now a valuable treasure—one photograph of the iceberg later sold for $32,000.

2 WHYDAH GALLY
USA

Pirate captain "Black Sam" Bellamy (1689–1717) sailed up the Massachusetts coast in the captured ship, *Whydah*, before it sank in a violent storm. The crew and their prisoners were mostly killed in the storm, and a few surviving crewmen were captured and hanged. The ship lay undisturbed for more than 260 years. Its discovery in 1984 was made with the aid of a genuine map from the 1700s. It was the first time a real pirate ship had been found and identified by name.

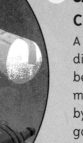

3 SAN JOSÉ
Colombia

A robotic submarine officially discovered the wreck of this galleon, belonging to King Philip V of Spain, more than 300 years after it was sunk by British sailors. The Colombian government has kept its precise location secret because the wreck is thought to contain gold, silver, and emeralds worth billions of dollars.

4 NUESTRA SEÑORA DE LAS MERCEDES
Spain

An incredible 18 tons (17 tonnes) of precious gold and silver coins were found near the wreck of this Spanish warship off the coast of Portugal. It is thought to have been carrying more than half a million silver coins when it was sunk by the British in 1804 during the Battle of Cape Santa Maria. The ship had been carrying goods and wealth back to Spain from its empire in South America.

5 **MARY ROSE**
UK

The pride of English King Henry VIII's navy, the *Mary Rose* was a successful battleship for more than thirty years but then sank in 1545. In 1982 around sixty million people watched on television as the wreck of its hull was raised up from the depths. Since then, the bones of nearly 200 sailors and thousands of personal objects have been brought up by divers. The wreck and its contents have provided fascinating clues about life in England during the mid-1500s.

6 **NANKING CARGO**
Indonesia

British divers found 126 solid gold ingots and more than 150,000 pieces of traditional blue-and-white china on the wreck of the Dutch ship *Geldermalsen*, which sank in the 1700s. Most of the plates, bowls, and cups were not damaged, even after more than two centuries underwater. Keen collectors paid around $13 million for them when they were cleaned and put on sale.

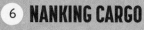

7 **CAESAREA TREASURE**
Israel

In 2015 a scuba diver swimming off the coast of Israel discovered an amazing hoard of more than 2,000 gold coins. This is by far the largest find of its kind in this part of the Mediterranean. Historians now know the coins are nearly 1,000 years old. A single one would have been equivalent to a month's pay for an ordinary soldier.

8 **BELITUNG SHIPWRECK**
Indonesia

This Arabian merchant's vessel, or dhow, sank on a voyage from China to the Middle East nearly twelve centuries ago. Archeologists have learned an enormous amount about how early boats were built by studying its wooden hull. They have also recovered the largest collection of Chinese Tang-dynasty objects ever found. This includes spice jars, a jug with a dragon's head spout, and even inkwells made more than 1,000 years ago.

FROM OTHER WORLDS

Some of our rarest treasures are truly out of this world. They could have come from outer space and be billions of years older than even the dinosaurs. Or we might even have built them ourselves to help us begin to explore the universe. If space travel becomes commonplace, these things might lose their value. But for now, we treasure them.

APOLLO 11 COMMAND MODULE
USA

More than 5,000 rockets have been blasted into space, and more than 500 men and women from more than forty different countries have traveled on board them. But only twelve people have ever flown all the way to another world. They had the incredible experience of standing on the Moon's surface and gazing back at Earth, nearly 240,000 miles (400,000 km) away.

The twelve astronauts were part of the USA's Apollo program. These missions into space were the most complex and most expensive engineering challenges in human history. The first astronauts to step onto the Moon were Neil Armstrong and Buzz Aldrin, who began their great adventure in the Saturn V, the largest, most powerful rocket ever flown.

Only this tiny capsule completed the return journey. You can see it today on display at the Smithsonian National Air and Space Museum in Washington, D.C. It's a unique and extraordinary tribute not just to the courageous astronauts but to the more than 400,000 scientists and engineers who worked for years to get them to the Moon safely—and home again when their mission was complete.

Moon rocks

The astronauts on the Apollo program also brought back other treasures: samples from the surface of the Moon. Scientists have studied these in order to learn about our cosmic neighbor. But since their arrival on Earth, around 180 moon rocks have gone missing. Many have probably been sold in secret to collectors for a high price.

HOBA METEORITE
Namibia

The Hoba meteorite is a 66-ton (60-tonne) lump of space rock that crashed down to Earth less than 80,000 years ago. Unusually it remained in one piece when it landed, possibly because its wide, flat surfaces helped it to slow down as it fell from the sky. It was only discovered about a century ago when a farmer came across it while out hunting.

Although it has now been completely uncovered, it's so heavy that nobody has even tried to move it. But over the years, several pieces have been chipped off and stolen. One 5.5-pound (2.5-kg) wedge was even presented to the British Museum. The meteorite is now a protected monument and a popular tourist attraction in the region of southern Africa where it sits.

Heavyweight
The Hoba meteorite weighs around the same as five double-decker London buses. When it hit Earth, it was traveling a lot faster than a jet plane.

Gifts from outer space
Meteorites have been crashing down on Earth ever since its formation 4.5 billion years ago. It may be that they brought with them an even more precious treasure, something none of us could live without—water! Today, many scientists think that asteroids falling to the Earth as meteorites brought some of the water that made our planet the blue one we know today.

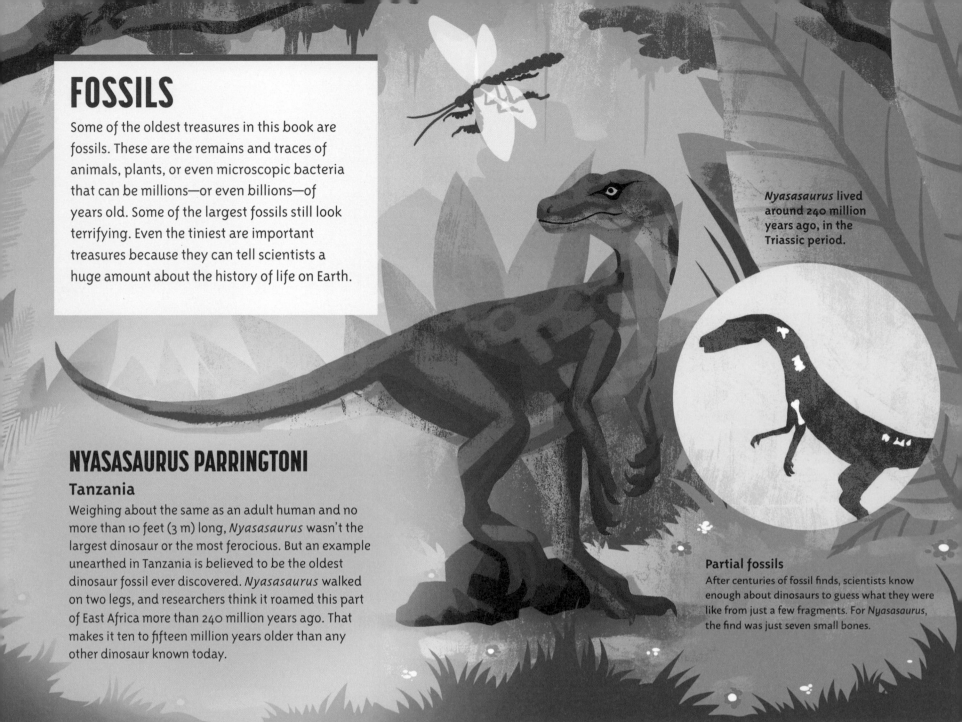

FOSSILS

Some of the oldest treasures in this book are fossils. These are the remains and traces of animals, plants, or even microscopic bacteria that can be millions—or even billions—of years old. Some of the largest fossils still look terrifying. Even the tiniest are important treasures because they can tell scientists a huge amount about the history of life on Earth.

Nyasasaurus lived around 240 million years ago, in the Triassic period.

NYASASAURUS PARRINGTONI

Tanzania

Weighing about the same as an adult human and no more than 10 feet (3 m) long, *Nyasasaurus* wasn't the largest dinosaur or the most ferocious. But an example unearthed in Tanzania is believed to be the oldest dinosaur fossil ever discovered. *Nyasasaurus* walked on two legs, and researchers think it roamed this part of East Africa more than 240 million years ago. That makes it ten to fifteen million years older than any other dinosaur known today.

Partial fossils
After centuries of fossil finds, scientists know enough about dinosaurs to guess what they were like from just a few fragments. For *Nyasasaurus*, the find was just seven small bones.

YANJI DINOSAURS

China

One of the world's great dinosaur experts, or palaeontologists, is Xu Xing of the Chinese Academy of Sciences in Beijing. He has made some remarkable discoveries on building sites in the city of Yanji in eastern China. When workmen were digging the foundations for new buildings, Xu found four ancient skeletons. Three were from crocodiles, and one was from a type of sauropod, the largest plant-eating dinosaurs. Even after millions of years, these unique specimens are in such good condition that a new museum is being created to put them on display.

BURGESS SHALE

Canada

For more than a century, this area of softer rock in the Canadian Rocky Mountains has been famous for the remarkable fossils found there. They are the remains of plants and animals that got buried in gooey mud about half a billion years ago. One of the strangest animals, *Opabinia*, has five eyes and a long nose like a vacuum cleaner. Another, *Hallucigenia*, looks like a worm with sharp spines. Some of the Burgess Shale specimens are so well preserved that scientists can actually tell what the creature ate for its final meal.

A strange, underwater world

The animals and other organisms discovered at the Burgess Shale are very different from most that exist today. In many cases, scientists still aren't sure if the specimens have living relatives. But careful study has shown that 500 million years ago, in the Cambrian period, there was already a familiar mix of grazers, scavengers, and fierce predators.

Olenoides
A trilobite, a hard-shelled animal

Wiwaxia
A grazing animal with scales and spines

Aysheaia
A relative of velvet worms

Anomalocaris
A dangerous predator

Opabinia
A five-eyed animal

SACRED TREASURES

Great churches and temples, tiny chapels, ancient priests' tombs, and holy books have always been precious treasures to religious followers. Some religious communities have even protected and worshipped the bones of saints, although it can be impossible to prove that they are really genuine.

BIRMINGHAM QURAN

Egypt

Muslims believe that God revealed the words of their holiest book, the Quran, to the Prophet Muhammad. Sadly, a couple of pages may be all that survive of the oldest known copy. It was written in ink on sheep- or goatskin at least 1,370 years ago, which means that it could even have been produced in Muhammad's lifetime. It was probably kept at a mosque—a Muslim place of worship—in Egypt for most of its history. While most of the book has been lost, these two remaining pages are kept at the University of Birmingham in the UK. They form part of an important collection of 3,000 Middle Eastern manuscripts.

TOPKAPI RELICS

Turkey

For centuries many people believed that treasures called "relics" associated with their favorite saints and prophets had miraculous or healing powers. Saints' bones, and even their blood, were kept in luxurious gold containers. Other relics were just everyday things that were believed to have belonged to people mentioned in religious books. A museum in Istanbul called Topkapi—once a Sultan's palace—still has several examples of these relics. They include a bowl belonging to the biblical Abraham, a sword belonging to King David (who, according to the Hebrew Bible, killed Goliath), and a staff or stick said to have been carried by the prophet Moses when he led the Israelites out of Egypt. But perhaps most unusual of all is a piece of the Muslim prophet Muhammad's tooth.

DIAMOND SUTRA

India

No one knows for sure when this important Buddhist manuscript was first written. However, we do know that by the 400s CE it had already been translated into Chinese from Sanskrit, the Indian language it was composed in. Since then it has been translated into many more languages, so it has been read by people from many different countries. These include Japan, Korea, Mongolia, Vietnam, and Tibet. One of the best copies is a Chinese one kept in the British Library. It was printed using engraved wooden blocks and has a date on it: May 11, 868 CE. This makes it the world's earliest complete and dated printed book.

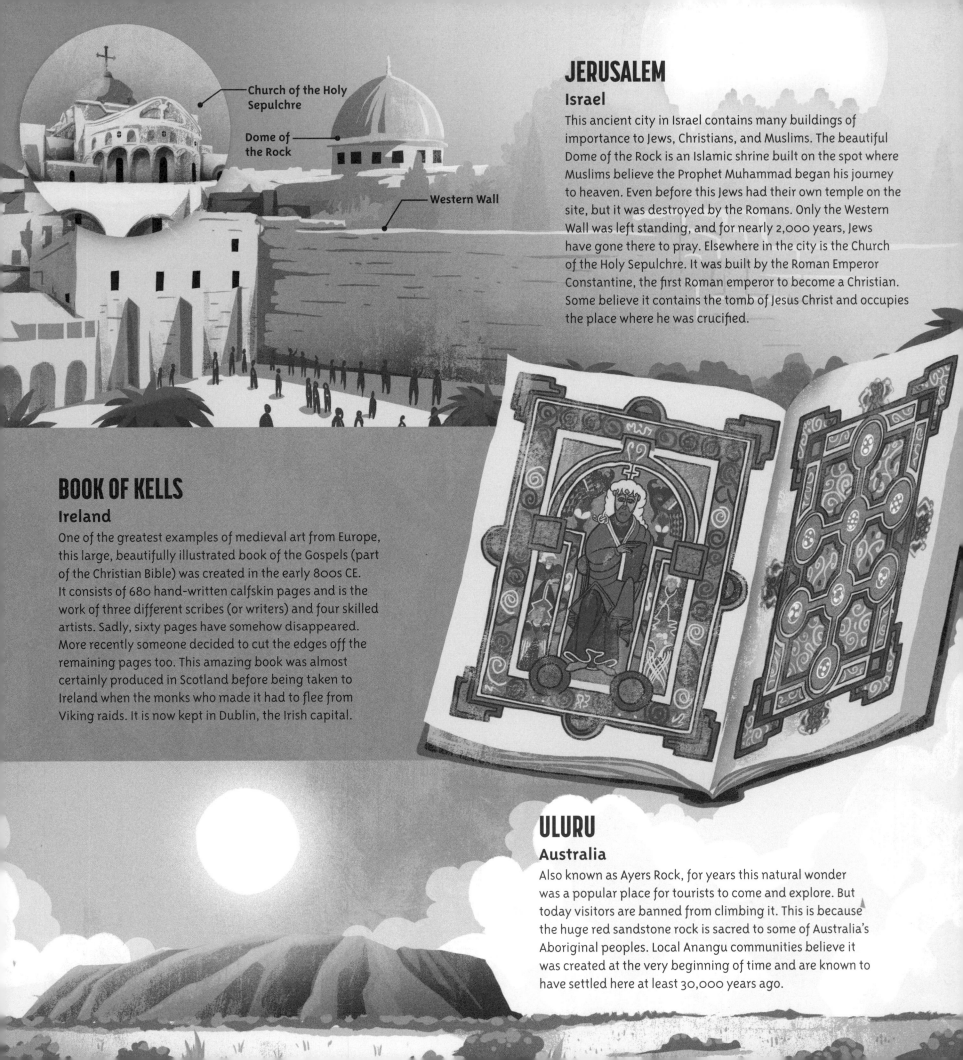

Church of the Holy Sepulchre

Dome of the Rock

Western Wall

JERUSALEM
Israel

This ancient city in Israel contains many buildings of importance to Jews, Christians, and Muslims. The beautiful Dome of the Rock is an Islamic shrine built on the spot where Muslims believe the Prophet Muhammad began his journey to heaven. Even before this Jews had their own temple on the site, but it was destroyed by the Romans. Only the Western Wall was left standing, and for nearly 2,000 years, Jews have gone there to pray. Elsewhere in the city is the Church of the Holy Sepulchre. It was built by the Roman Emperor Constantine, the first Roman emperor to become a Christian. Some believe it contains the tomb of Jesus Christ and occupies the place where he was crucified.

BOOK OF KELLS
Ireland

One of the greatest examples of medieval art from Europe, this large, beautifully illustrated book of the Gospels (part of the Christian Bible) was created in the early 800s CE. It consists of 680 hand-written calfskin pages and is the work of three different scribes (or writers) and four skilled artists. Sadly, sixty pages have somehow disappeared. More recently someone decided to cut the edges off the remaining pages too. This amazing book was almost certainly produced in Scotland before being taken to Ireland when the monks who made it had to flee from Viking raids. It is now kept in Dublin, the Irish capital.

ULURU
Australia

Also known as Ayers Rock, for years this natural wonder was a popular place for tourists to come and explore. But today visitors are banned from climbing it. This is because the huge red sandstone rock is sacred to some of Australia's Aboriginal peoples. Local Anangu communities believe it was created at the very beginning of time and are known to have settled here at least 30,000 years ago.

BIG AND SMALL TREASURES

Treasures can be very large or very small, but their value often isn't related to their size. Sometimes no one can say how much a treasure is worth. Unless something is put up for sale, it's impossible to put an accurate price on it. Many treasures never will be sold, so we just call them "priceless."

LESHAN GIANT BUDDHA
China

The ancient world's tallest statue, this enormous figure of Buddha was carved out of a cliff in China in the 700s CE. The Buddha is shown sitting down but is still more than 230 feet (70 m) tall—about the same height as a 20-story building. The statue is carved out of red sandstone, a type of rock that is quite soft. A clever drainage system built inside the Buddha has protected the soft rock from rainwater damage for more than 1,000 years.

An even bigger Buddha

Colossal statues of the Buddha can be found across Southeast Asia and China. The tallest today, the Spring Temple Buddha in China, was completed in 2009 and is 420 ft (128 m) tall—115 ft (35 m) taller than the Statue of Liberty—making it the second tallest statue in the world after the Statue of Unity in India.

MONA LISA
France

The most famous painting in the world is surprisingly small—only 30 inches (77 cm) high and 21 inches (53 cm) wide—but this single painting could be worth almost a billion dollars or more. No one can be certain about its exact value because it hasn't been bought or sold since the 1500s. The portrait, by Italian artist Leonardo da Vinci, originally belonged to a French king and later to the French emperor Napoleon. People have tried to damage the painting at least three times by throwing objects at it or spraying it with paint. It has even been stolen once, and it took two years to get it back. Today it is displayed behind thick, bulletproof glass in the Louvre Museum in Paris. A law has been passed making it impossible for anyone to sell the painting.

Marvelous museum

The Louvre Museum in Paris, where the Mona Lisa is housed, is the biggest art museum in the world. Today, it displays almost 40,000 works of art. Once a grand palace for royalty, it was turned into a museum in the late 1700s when France's kings were overthrown.

Mini Lisa

The *Mona Lisa* has been copied many times in different forms. Some artists have challenged themselves to re-create it in truly tiny form. *Mona Lisa* copies have been made from microscopic bacteria or by putting together tiny clusters of molecules. One artist even painted a portrait of the *Mona Lisa* no bigger than a pinhead, using one of his own eyelashes.

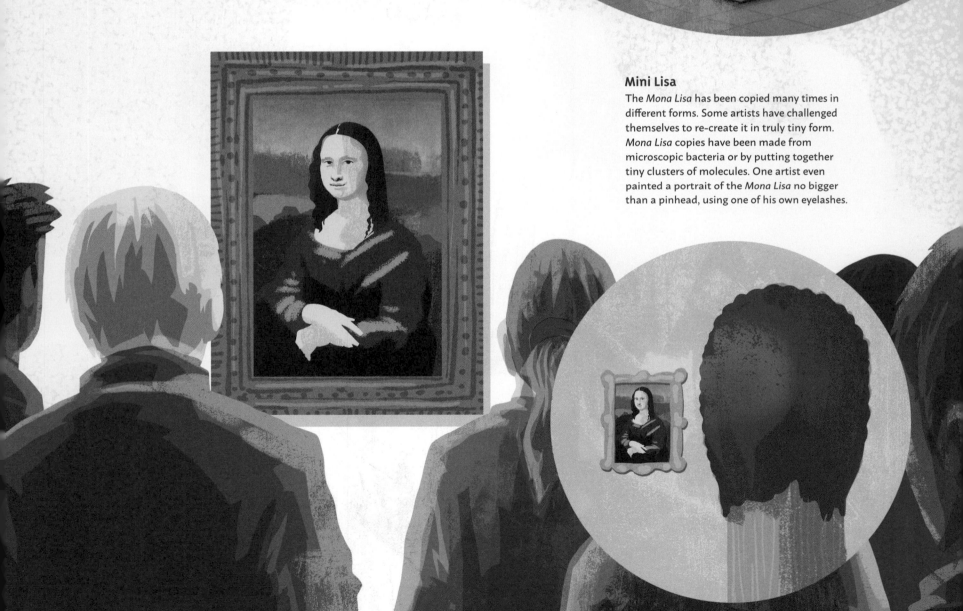

TIKAL

Guatemala

The Maya people have lived in this part of what is now Guatemala, in Central America, since around 3,500 years ago. Using only stone tools (metal was rare and expensive) the ancient Maya built advanced cities, as the magnificent ruins at Tikal show. It was one of their largest and most important cities. The ancient Maya had complicated religious rituals, and the ruins at Tikal include the remains of five stone pyramids and many fabulous stone temples. The city was once home to up to 100,000 people, and the ruins now cover an area of about 6 square miles (15 square km).

Ancient book
The Dresden Codex is the oldest surviving Maya book. It is around 800 years old.

Many Maya could read and write. They studied the stars and mathematics, and developed their own music and architectural style. The Maya were some of the first people in the world to drink chocolate and believed that cacao seeds, also called cocoa beans, were a gift from the gods. Big noses were considered attractive in Maya society, so some rich Maya used makeup to make their noses look even bigger!

The Temple of the Great Jaguar is a huge stepped pyramid nearly 165 feet (50 m) tall. It was built as a tomb for Jasaw Chan K'awiil I, who ruled Tikal about 1,300 years ago. When it was finished, it was topped with a giant roof structure decorated with a carving of the king on his throne. Unfortunately, the image has now disappeared. Archeologists have found many precious items in a burial chamber inside the pyramid. They include carved animal bones, bowls, and ornaments made from seashells and jade, a valuable green stone. Long ago, the bowls may have contained food and drink for the dead king.

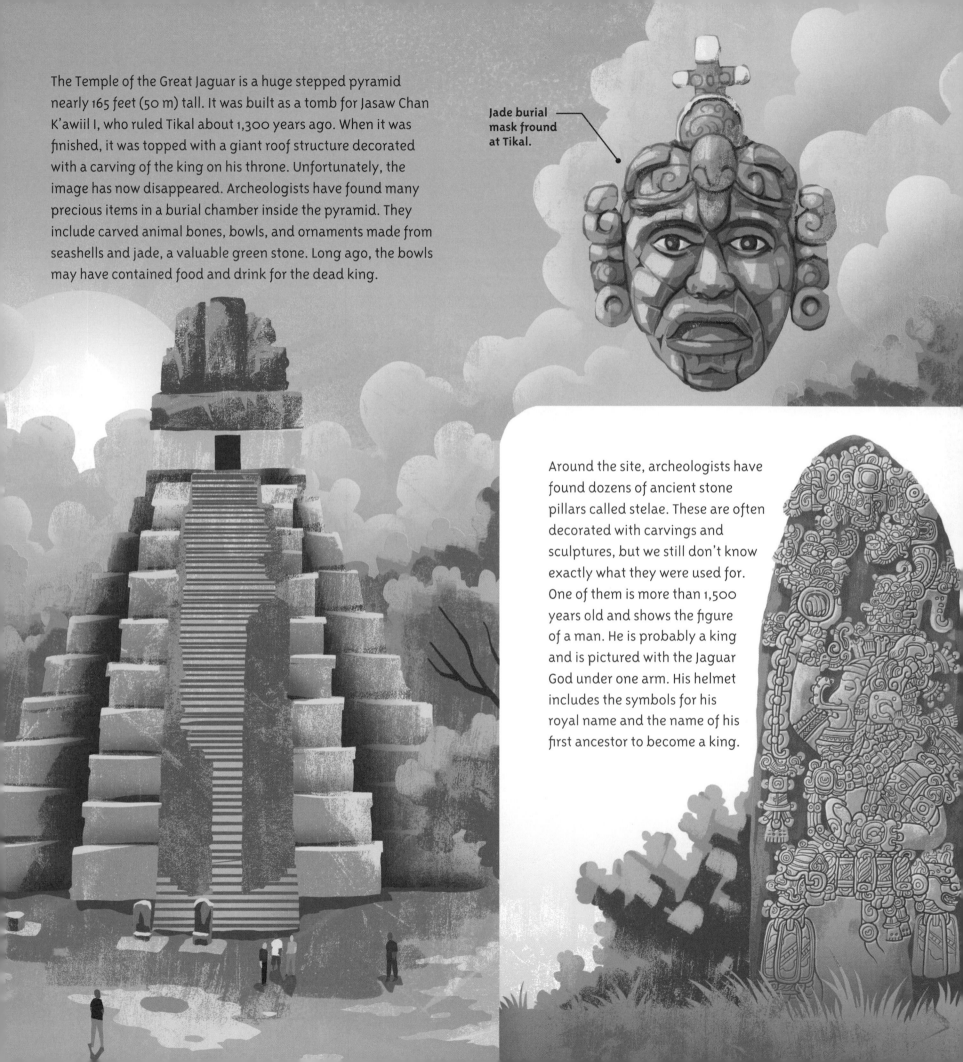

Jade burial mask fround at Tikal.

Around the site, archeologists have found dozens of ancient stone pillars called stelae. These are often decorated with carvings and sculptures, but we still don't know exactly what they were used for. One of them is more than 1,500 years old and shows the figure of a man. He is probably a king and is pictured with the Jaguar God under one arm. His helmet includes the symbols for his royal name and the name of his first ancestor to become a king.

ARCHITECTURAL WONDERS

Some of the greatest buildings in history now lie in ruins, but others have survived for hundreds or even thousands of years. Still standing after earthquakes, wars, and revolutions, buildings like these now attract millions of visitors every year.

HAGIA SOPHIA
Turkey

When the Christian city of Constantinople was invaded by Muslim soldiers in 1453, its most important church, Hagia Sophia, was converted into a mosque. At around this time, people also began calling the city Istanbul. From the 300s to the 1200s, Constantinople had been one of the richest cities in the world. Its powerful rulers had designed Hagia Sophia to look spectacular. Nearly 1,500 years after it was built, this incredible structure still towers high over the city, although it has now been converted into a museum.

Islamic history
The tall towers around Hagia Sophia are minarets. These are found on mosques, and they allow the call to prayer to be heard from far away.

Central location
The city of Istanbul occupies a unique space between Europe and Asia. For thousands of years, goods from as far away as China, India, and northern Europe were traded there, making it one of the most vibrant cities in history.

Lavish interior
The expansive interior of Hagia Sophia includes several smaller rooms and domes, all built around a central large dome and decorated with stunning gold mosaics. This central dome is an incredible 102 ft (31 m) wide.

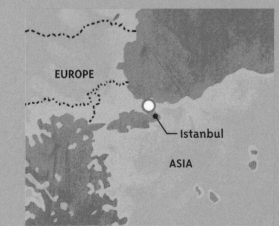

EUROPE

Istanbul

ASIA

TAJ MAHAL

India

This incredible building is the huge and lavish tomb of the emperor Shah Jahan (1592–1666) and one of his nine wives, Mumtaz Mahal. It is built of beautiful ivory-white marble and took 20,000 people about twenty-two years to complete. A thousand elephants were needed to carry the marble. The final cost is very hard to estimate but might have been equivalent to more than 50 billion Indian rupees or about $730 million. Originally the finial, or spike, on top of the main dome was made of real gold, but the gold original was replaced by a bronze copy in the 1800s.

Powerful ruler

Shah Jahan was emperor of the Mughals, who ruled over what are now India and Pakistan from the 1500s to the 1800s.

Master builders

At the top of the dome is a large hole called the oculus, which means "eye" in Latin, the language of ancient Rome. This lets sunlight into the building (there are no windows), but it means that visitors can get wet when it rains.

PANTHEON

Italy

This famous ancient Roman temple eventually became a Christian church. Its most incredible feature is its domed roof—nearly 2,000 years after it was built, this dome is still the largest concrete structure of its type in the world. It weighs more than 4,960 tons (4,500 tonnes), but it doesn't need any beams or rods to hold it up.

M·AGRIPPA·L·F·COS·T·TIVM·FECIT

VERSAILLES

France

Louis XIV ruled for 72 years and 110 days (longer than any other French king) and built his country's largest and most luxurious palace just outside the capital city, Paris. Surprisingly, ordinary members of the public were allowed to come and visit—but they were only allowed in if they were well dressed. Guards were ordered to send them away if they weren't.

Grand palace

By the end of Louis XIV's reign, Versailles had more than 700 rooms, 1,252 chimneys, and 67 staircases. Its park and gardens covered an extraordinary 30 square miles (80 square km) and contained 1,400 fountains.

TOMB RAIDERS

For centuries, it was a tradition for powerful kings and queens to be buried with their favorite jewels and other precious objects. Knowing this, tomb raiders have often broken into these graves. Sometimes they are treasure hunters who rob the grave site. Other times a tomb remains undisturbed until archeologists discover it many years later.

TOMB OF MARQUIS YI OF ZENG
China

The grave of the Marquis Yi of Zeng was discovered by Chinese soldiers. Marquis Yi died in the 400s BCE and was buried with many treasures, including several fascinating musical instruments. The largest, the bianzhong, is made of sixty-four bells and would have been played by five people using wooden mallets. The most unusual are the shengs. These were made using a type of fruit called a gourd that had grown in a particular shape. The fruit was dried and hollowed out so it could be blown to make notes.

HEUNEBURG IRON AGE TOMB
Germany

This grave of an Iron Age woman was found on the site of an old hill-fort more than 2,600 years after she died. No one knows who she was, but her grave contained many precious items. These included amber and gold jewelry, leather belts and furs, bronze armor for a horse, and objects made from the horns of wild boar. Two fossils found in the grave may have been used in religious rituals, so it is possible she was an important priestess.

TERRA-COTTA ARMY
China

In 1974 farmers digging a new well discovered massive pits containing more than 7,000 life-sized human figures, along with 130 chariots and nearly 700 figures of horses. This "army" was created to protect the nearby tomb of China's first emperor, Qin Shi Huang. Each figure was made of a dried clay called terra-cotta more than 2,200 years ago. Then it was decorated using paint made from ground-up bones (for white) or minerals and precious stones (for the other colors). Because of its immense size, the army is widely regarded as one of the greatest archeological discoveries of the last century.

TUTANKHAMUN'S TOMB

Egypt

The gold treasures found in an Egyptian tomb in 1922 were so spectacular that they have made the young "boy-king" Tutankhamun the most famous of all the ancient Egyptian pharaohs. Not much is known about him, but his grave is one of the richest that has ever been found in Egypt, although he was only a teenager when he died.

The journey to the afterlife

A mural painted on the north wall of the burial chamber depicts Tutankhamun's journey to the afterlife. According to the ancient Egyptian religion, this was a dangerous journey that took a long time. In the mural, Tutankhamun can be seen meeting the god Osiris and the goddess Nut along the way.

Nut

Pharaoh Tutankhamun dressed as the god Osiris

Osiris

A pharaoh's treasure

The most impressive treasure from the tomb is probably Tutankhamun's mask. It is made of solid gold and a bright blue stone called lapis lazuli. Recently, it had to be restored after somebody broke off its "beard" and then tried to stick it back on with glue. Several ornate model boats were also found in the tomb. The ancient Egyptians believed that they would be useful for transport in the afterlife.

Hieroglyphs

Ancient Egyptians used a system of pictures, called hieroglyphs, for writing their language. They can be found all over ancient Egyptian tombs, listing the deeds of the people buried there.

Pharaoh Tutankhamun's name in hieroglyphics

BY OFFICIAL DECREE

Even before most people could read and write, written documents were an important way for powerful rulers to ensure that their laws were understood and obeyed. They had to be produced by scribes, because many early kings and queens were no better at writing than anyone else.

DOMESDAY BOOK

UK

This was a huge book produced shortly after the Norman invasion of England in 1066. Containing around two million words, it is a record of everything that anyone in the country owned at the time. This includes animals as well as land and even farmworkers, who were often treated as if they belonged to the local lord. The book helped the new king, William the Conqueror, to understand how rich his people were. Now William could figure out how much tax they had to pay him! This made the book extremely unpopular at the time, but it has helped modern historians understand life in the Middle Ages.

Local landmark
The edicts were written on large stones and pillars and dotted around Ashoka's empire. They were written in three different languages, to ensure local people could read them.

EDICTS OF ASHOKA

South Asia

Carved into stones and pillars spread across parts of India, Bangladesh, Nepal, Afghanistan, and Pakistan, the Edicts of Ashoka are a bit like the Ten Commandments in the Bible. Emperor Ashoka ruled this region from around 268 to 232 BCE, and the Edicts were the laws he wanted people to obey after he became a Buddhist. Ashoka's Edicts told people to stop killing animals and being cruel to prisoners. Everyone was ordered to respect all religions as well, not just their own, and not to try to become famous.

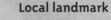

ROSETTA STONE
Egypt

This large black stone is kept in the British Museum in London and is more than 2,200 years old. The writing on it is an official message from a council of priests praising the pharaoh Ptolemy V Epiphanes. Because the writing is in two different languages and three different scripts, the stone's discovery in 1799 made it possible to understand ancient Egyptian writing, called hieroglyphics. Before the Rosetta Stone was found, the pictures used in this writing were like a secret code that no one could understand.

hieroglyphic writing

Demotic writing

ancient Greek writing

Name of the pharoah

A cartouche was a set of symbols that was used to write royal names in hieroglyphics. The cartouche of the pharoah Ptolemy V can be found on the Rosetta Stone.

MAGNA CARTA
UK

When King John upset England's most powerful barons in the early 1200s they made him put his seal on a document promising to obey the law and rule in a fair way. The document was called Magna Carta, which means "Great Charter" in Latin. It was the first time a king of England had been treated in this way. John didn't like it and a war briefly broke out between him and the barons. However, the king died before the war could go very far. A copy of Magna Carta is kept at the British Library, and some of its sections are still important parts of British law today.

Kings and queens

Nobles

Knights

Peasants

Feudal system

Medieval kings and queens ruled through the "feudal system." This meant they held all the power and could do what they wanted. The nobles, knights, and, finally, peasants were all below them. Magna Carta was one of the first times people had put a limit on a ruler's power.

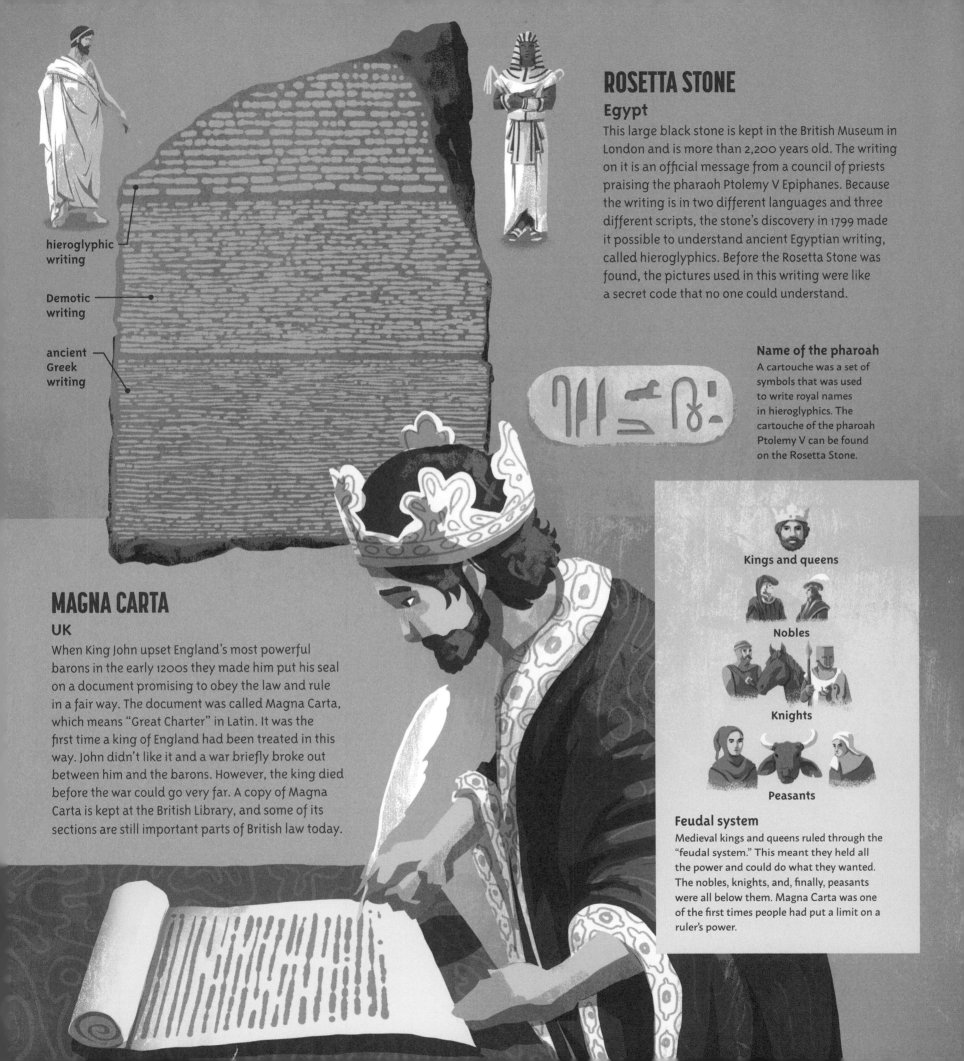

COLLECTORS

Sometimes treasures are kept together in a collection. This could belong to a single individual, or be open to the public for all to see. Either way, collections house some of the most fascinating and unusual treasures in the world.

ROYAL PHILATELIC COLLECTION
UK

Someone who collects rare stamps is called a philatelist. One of the most successful was King George V of the UK who lived from 1865 to 1936 and collected stamps from all over the British Empire. He once paid £1,450 (about $190,000 today) for a single stamp. At the time, a house in London could be bought for just £300. King George kept the stamp in one of 328 large red stamp albums. King George VI later added numerous blue albums to the collection, and his daughter, Queen Elizabeth II, has carried on the tradition with green ones. No one knows how much the whole collection is worth, but the stamp George V paid so much for has been valued at $2.6 million. When it was brand new, it would have only cost about two cents.

RANCHO OBI-WAN STAR WARS COLLECTION
USA

Around the world, millions of people collect *Star Wars* toys. But no one has a larger collection than Steve Sansweet. The American film enthusiast started collecting when he was 31, and before long he had more than 300,000 different items. His collection includes action figures, books, and clothing, but also items that were actually used in the films. A special museum in California now houses the collection so that fans can visit.

STRADIVARIUS STRINGED INSTRUMENTS
Italy

Musicians agree that the best violins ever produced were made in Italy by Antonio Stradivari, also called Stradivarius. From 1666 until his death in 1737, he made stringed instruments such as violas, harps, and cellos—but his violins are the most famous. Even after more than two centuries, 500 or so of his violins still exist. The highest price ever paid for one is $16 million, and many of them are now kept in museums or private collections. The Palacio Real museum in Madrid, Spain, has the largest collection open to the public, with a viola, a cello and two violins. But some of Stradivarius's instruments are still played regularly, lent by generous owners to the world's top musicians.

SCHLUMPF COLLECTION
France

Bugattis are some of the rarest and most valuable cars in the world. Beginning in 1909 this French carmaker built top-speed racing cars, as well as the "Royale," a car so luxurious that even most kings couldn't afford to buy one. Hans and Fritz Schlumpf bought two of them—but then, these two Swiss brothers were probably the most obsessive Bugatti collectors ever. In a single year, they bought nearly fifty Bugattis, and soon after bought another thirty from a rival enthusiast. It's no surprise that they eventually ran out of money. Their cars now belong to France's National Motor Museum.

LA SPECOLA
Italy

The world's largest and most important collection of wax anatomical specimens belongs to the oldest scientific museum in Europe, which opened in 1775. It was the first such museum to let the public visit. Many of the wax models are of dead people and were made to help medical students understand how the human body worked. In some countries, using real dead bodies was against the law (and even where it wasn't, bodies quickly began to rot). Instead, life-size models of men and women were made using wax. These highly realistic models can be very gruesome when the bodies are shown cut open or suffering from some horrible disease.

ROCKS AND GEMSTONES

Some of the most valuable treasures on Earth are minerals and gems dug up from the ground. Often these are cut and polished to make them into jewels, but even a collection of uncut gemstones is a valuable find.

SMITHSONIAN GEM AND MINERAL COLLECTION
USA

One of the world's largest collections of rocks and minerals, this treasure trove has nearly 600,000 different specimens. It includes 45,000 pieces of meteorite from outer space and an incredible 10,000 precious gems. Scientists and geologists use the collection for research, but every month thousands of visitors come just to see the famous Hope Diamond, a deep blue stone about the size of a walnut. This gemstone belonged to King Louis XVI of France and may have been worn by his queen, Marie Antoinette. Because both were later executed in a gruesome way during the French Revolution, many people think the stone is cursed.

Gold

Quartz

Beryl

Hope diamond

Whitney Flame topaz

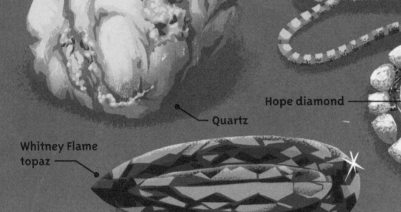

Amethyst quartz

Precious collection
The Smithsonian collection includes a variety of valuable gemstones, such as diamonds and emeralds. Others, such as quartz and beryl, are remarkable for their incredible patterns and shapes.

Georgina emerald

Chalk emerald

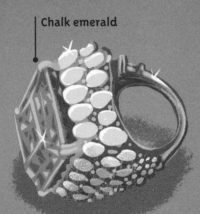

Far-flung places
The meteorite collection includes several rocks from Mars. These rocks were blasted out into space from Mars by a meteorite, and then eventually came crashing down on Earth. Scientists have studied the meteorites to learn more about the planet's past and the origins of our solar system.

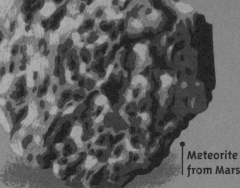

Meteorite from Mars

Frederick Wells, holding the uncut diamond, who ran the mine where it was found.

The Imperial State Crown and Sovereign's Sceptre with Cross. Both are part of the crown jewels of the UK and contain gemstones cut from the Cullinan Diamond.

THE CULLINAN DIAMOND

UK

The largest diamond ever discovered was found just 30 feet (9 m) below the surface in South Africa in 1905. It weighed more than 1.3 pounds (600 g) and was presented to a British king, Edward VII. The king had it cut into more than 100 different gems. They now form part of the British Crown Jewels. The largest gems are in the Imperial State Crown and a scepter. It's impossible to say how much these are now worth, but in 1905 the mine owner was paid £150,000 for the original diamond. That's more than $19.5 million in today's currency.

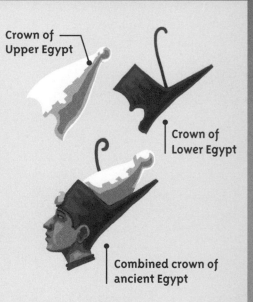

Royal symbols

Crowns and other royal jewels are powerful symbols. Many are decorated with expensive gems and metals to show the wealth and power of the king or queen. The crown of ancient Egypt, shown here, combined the crowns of Upper and Lower Egypt to show the pharaoh had power over both.

Crown of Upper Egypt

Crown of Lower Egypt

Combined crown of ancient Egypt

GLOSSARY

AMBER
Hard orange material formed from a sticky liquid produced by trees long ago and hardened over time. Used in jewelry and other decorative objects.

ANTIQUE
Something old that is particularly special because of its age or the way in which it has been made.

ARCHEOLOGIST
Someone who digs up ancient artifacts or the remains of living things to study human beings' past.

ARCHITECTURE
The study of buildings. Also, the process of designing buildings or the features of particular buildings.

ARTIFACT
An object made by humans, usually long ago.

ASTEROID
Rocky object orbiting the sun, smaller than a dwarf planet.

AZTEC
Culture and empire that developed in what is today northern Mexico, beginning in the 1300s. The Aztec Empire ruled a large area but came to an end following a Spanish invasion in 1521.

BARON
Lowest rank of British noble.

BIBLE
Holy book of the Christian religion. The Bible includes the Old and New Testaments. The Old Testament also corresponds to the some of the principal holy texts of Judaism.

BRONZE
Shiny orange-brown metal made by combining copper and tin.

BRONZE AGE
The period following the Stone Age in European, Asian, and Middle Eastern history. During this period, bronze began to be used for making tools, weapons, and other objects.

BUDDHIST
Someone who follows the religion of Buddhism, which was established by a teacher most commonly called Buddha who lived in what is now Nepal around 500 BCE.

BURIAL MOUND
Man-made pile of earth and stones placed over a body as a burial site.

CARAT
Unit of weight used to measure gemstones and precious metals. One carat is equivalent to 200 mg (0.007 oz).

CHINA (MATERIAL)
Very hard but brittle material usually used for making dinnerware objects such as cups and plates. Also called porcelain. China is made by heating a mixture of clay and minerals at high temperatures.

CLIMATE CHANGE
Change of Earth's climate over time, in particular due to changes in Earth's atmosphere.

CLOCKWORK
Types of machine that use gears, wheels, and springs to function. Clockwork machines must be wound up to start them working.

CONSTELLATION
Group of stars that forms a pattern in the sky and that has been given a name.

CURRENCY
The types of money used in a particular place or country, or at a particular time.

EDICT
Order given by a powerful person, such as an emperor.

EPIDEMIC
Disease that spreads very quickly to lots of people and places.

GEOLOGIST
Someone who studies what the Earth is made of and how it changes over time.

GLOBAL WARMING
Steady increase in air temperature at or close to Earth's surface over the last approximately 200 years.

HINDU
Someone who follows the ancient and varied religion of Hinduism, which has its roots in India and has many gods and goddesses.

ICEBERG
Huge chunk of ice that floats in the sea or ocean. Icebergs are a dangerous obstacle to ships.

IRON AGE
Period following the Bronze Age in European, Asian, and Middle Eastern history. During this period, iron began to replace bronze as the primary material used for tools, weapons, and other objects.

INCA
Large South American empire that covered territories stretching from the Andes Mountains in today's Peru down the coast of what is today Chile. The Inca Empire began to expand around the middle of the 1400s, and lasted until around 1532, when it was destroyed by Spanish invaders.

JADE
Types of green gemstones mostly used for decoration and jewelry.

LLAMA
Woolly, grazing mammals from South America, related to camels.

LIMESTONE
Widely-found rocks made from a chemical compound called calcium carbonate, which usually originates from the shells of prehistoric animals.

LOOT
Steal things from somewhere, in particular during a war or raid.

MAMMOTH
Group of extinct elephant-like mammals once found on almost every continent. The enormous woolly mammoth lived in Northern Europe, North America, and Asia and is the most well known.

MANUSCRIPT
A handwritten piece of writing or music, or the original copy of a piece of writing or music.

MARBLE
Limestone that has been hardened further by extreme heat or pressure. Marble has been a popular decoration for lavish buildings and statues, due to its colorful patterns and shiny surface when polished.

MICROBE
Microscopic organisms, including bacteria, viruses, and many types of fungus.

MOSAIC
A decorative design made from lots of tiny pieces, such as stones, tiles, or shells, that together form a picture or pattern.

NAVY
Collection of ships and other vessels for fighting on the water or underwater.

NORMANS
Group of peoples who settled in northern France in the region that is now Normandy. The first Normans were Vikings from northern Europe. Normans traveled by ship conquering territories, including southern Italy, Sicily, and England, where they installed themselves as rulers.

PALEONTOLOGIST
Someone who studies fossilized animals, plants, and other other living things.

PAPYRUS
Paper-like material used in ancient times for writing on. Papyrus is made by pressing together and drying out the stems of the papyrus plant, a reed that grows in marshy areas such as the Nile River delta in Egypt.

PHARAOH
Principal ancient Egyptian ruler, similar to a king or queen.

PLASTER
Material made by mixing minerals and water, shaping the pasty mixture and allowing it to harden as it dries out. Plaster is used as a building material and for making or copying artworks.

REVOLUTION
Sudden and significant change in a government or society.

SAINT
Very holy person.

SARCOPHAGUS
Stone coffin for burying a body.

SCAVENGER
Animal that eats the bodies of already-dead animals.

SCEPTER
Ornamental staff held by a ruler that symbolizes their authority and power.

SHILLING
Coin once used as currency in the UK, Australia, New Zealand, Ireland, and Austria. Today, also the currency of Kenya, Somalia, Tanzania, and Uganda.

SHRINE
Holy place connected to a particular holy person, object, or event.

SIBERIA
Huge region of Russia that stretches from the Ural Mountains in the west to the Pacific Ocean in the east.

SILK
Very soft fabric made from fibers produced by silkworms, a type of moth.

SILK ROAD
Ancient route that connected China with Europe, allowing trade between the two regions and those in between.

SOLAR ECLIPSE
Event caused by the Moon passing between the Earth and Sun. During a solar eclipse, the Moon briefly blocks out the Sun's light when viewed from Earth.

STONE AGE
Period in human development that saw the beginning of the production and use of stone tools by humans.

TAPESTRY
Decorative fabric made by weaving fibers into a picture or pattern.

TIDE
The steady cycle of changing sea level over time. The cycle takes place around twice every day.

TOMB
Large structure, often underground, for burying the dead.

VIKINGS
People from Scandinavia in Northern Europe known for traveling across the sea and raiding, in particular from the 800s to 1000s CE.

INDEX

SOURCES

Ancient History Encyclopedia (www.ancient.eu)

Antikythera Mechanism Research Project (www.antikythera-mechanism.gr)

"Thracian Art," Archaeological Museum Plovdiv (www.archaeologicalmuseumplovdiv.org)

Atlas Obscura (www.atlasobscura.com)

"Australia's top 7 Aboriginal rock art sites," *Australian Geographic* (www.australiangeographic.com.au)

Bayeux museum (www.bayeuxmuseum.com)

BBC Bitesize (www.bbc.co.uk)

"The Birmingham Qu'ran," University of Birmingham (www.birmingham.ac.uk)

Blumberg, J. "A Brief History of the Amber Room," *Smithsonian Magazine* (www.smithsonianmag.com)

"Lascaux Cave," Bradshaw Foundation (www.bradshawfoundation.com)

"Gutenberg Bible," British Library (www.bl.uk)

"Printed copy of the Diamond Sutra," British Library (www.bl.uk)

"Shakespeare's First Folio," British Library (www.bl.uk)

British Museum (www.britishmuseum.org)

"Archaeologies of the Greek Past: Mask of 'Agamemnon'," Brown University (www.brown.edu)

"History," Bugatti (www.bugatti.com)

Cahokia Mounds (cahokiamounds.org)

"Imagine discovering the world's largest diamond, the Cullinan," Cape Town Diamond Museum (www.capetowndiamondmuseum.org)

Cartwright, J. & Nakamura, H. "What kind of a wave is Hokusai's Great wave off Kanagawa?," *Notes and Records of the Royal Society*, 63(2):119-135, May 2009 (London: The Royal Society)

Chateau de Versailles (www.chateauversailles.fr)

"The Forbidden City, Beijing — All You Want To Know," China Highlights (www.chinahighlights.com)

Cité de l'Automobile (www.citedelautomobile.com)

Cloos, E. "Domesday book — a brief material history," The National Archives (www.nationalarchives.gov.uk)

Covington, R. "Lost & Found," *Smithsonian Magazine* (www.smithsonianmag.com)

Crane, L. "Ettore Bugatti and the Schlumpf Brothers," *Hagerty* (www.hagerty.com)

"Svalbard Global Seed Vault," Crop Trust (www.croptrust.org)

Cullinan Diamond (www.cullinan-diamond.com)

Daley, J. "Five Things to Know About the Diamond Sutra, the World's Oldest Dates Printed Book," *Smithsonian Magazine* (www.smithsonianmag.com)

Daley, J. "New Exhibition Highlights Story of the Richest Man Who Ever Lived," *Smithsonian Magazine* (www.smithsonianmag.com)

David, A. "Hanukkah Gelt: 900-year-old Cache of Gold Coins Found in Ancient Israeli City of Caesarea," *Haaretz* (www.haaretz.com)

Davies, C. "Queen's prized £2m stamp to go on show," *The Telegraph* (www.telegraph.co.uk)

DKfindout! (www.dkfindout.com)

Encyclopaedia Britannica (www.britannica.com)

Eng, C. *Colours and Contrast: Ceramic Traditions in Chinese Architecture* (Leiden: Brill)

"Artist paints Mona Lisa miniature, using his eyelash," *Evening Standard* (www.standard.co.uk)

"The World of Fabergé," Fabergé (www.faberge.com)

"About the Great Barrier Reef," Great Barrier Reef (greatbarrierreef.org)

"The Smithsonian Gem and Mineral Collection," Gemological Institute of America (www.gia.edu)

Gilchrist, R. *Medieval Life: Archaeology and the Life Course* (2012, Woodbridge, UK: The Boydell Press)

"Boy unearths treasure of the Danish king Bluetooth in Germany," *The Guardian* (www.theguardian.com)

"Mexico City gold was Aztec loot Spanish abandoned as they fled in 1520, tests show," *The Guardian* (www.theguardian.com)

"China building boom uncovers buried dinosaurs, makes a star," *Gulf News* (gulfnews.com)

Guiness World Records (www.guinessworldrecords.com)

Gutenberg-Museum Mainz (www.gutenberg-museum.de)

Habermehl, N. "VOC Geldermalsen," Lost Treasures of the Seven Seas (www.oceantreasures.org)

Heather, P. "The Great Library of Alexandria?," *Library Philosophy and Practice* (2010)

History (www.history.com)

"Amber Room: Priceless Russian treasure stolen by Nazis 'discovered by German researchers'," *Independent* (www.independent.co.uk)

Indonesian gold: treasures from the National Museum, Jakarta (1999, Brisbane: Queensland Art Gallery)

"Hoba Meteorite," Info Namibia (www.info-namibia.com)

"Permanent exhibition Old Synagogue," Jewish Past and Present in Erfurt (juedisches-leben.erfurt.de)

Kennedy, M. "Hidden codex may reveal secrets of life in Mexico before Spanish conquest," *The Guardian* (www.theguardian.com)

Laliberté, M. "This Is the Most Heavily Guarded Place on the Planet," *Reader's Digest* (www.rd.com)

Lascaux (www.lascaux.fr)

Leithead, A. "Africa's oldest map unveiled," *BBC News* (news.bbc.co.uk)

Live Science (www.livescience.com)

The London Silver Vaults (silvervaultslondon.com)

"History of Palmyra," Lonely Planet (www.lonelyplanet.com)

"Forbidden City," Lonely Planet (www.lonelyplanet.com)

Louvre Museum (www.louvre.fr)

Löwenmensch Foundation (www.lowenmensch.org)

"Perito Moreno glacier," Los Glaciares National Park (www.losglaciares.com)

The Magna Carta Trust (magnacarta800th.com)

The Mary Rose (marose.org)

Melvin, S. "The Chimes of Ancient China," *The New York Times* (www.nytimes.com)

"La Salle des Taureaux," Ministère de la Culture (www.culture.gouv.fr)

"Knossos," Municipality of Heraklion (www.heraklion.gr)

"The Cheapside Hoard," Museum of London (www.museumoflondon.org)

"The Erfurt Treasure — The Story of a Ring," Museum of the Jewish People at Beit Hatfutsot (www.bh.org.il)

"What Was the Apollo Program?," NASA (www.nasa.gov)

National Geographic (www.nationalgeographic.com)

National Geographic Kids (www.natgeokids.com)

"Mammoth Cave," National Park Service (www.nps.gov)

"Quick Facts on Arctic Sea Ice," National Snow & Ice Data Center (nsidc.org)

Oak Island Treasure (www.oakislandtreasure.co.uk)

Online Etymology Dictionary (www.etymonline.com)

"About the Palace Museum," The Palace Museum (en.dpm.org.cn)

Paterson, T. "The 1,200-year-old sunken treasure that revealed an undiscovered China," *Independent* (www.independent.co.uk)

"Instrumentos musicales," Patrimonio Nacional (www.patrimonionacional.es)

Peck, T. "Stradivarius: Italian craftsmanship retains perfect pitch," *Independent* (www.independent.co.uk)

"The Bakhshali manuscript: The world's oldest zero?," Phys.org (phys.org)

Poole, R. M. "The tiny island with human-sized money," BBC (www.bbc.com)

Pound, C. "The Nazi art hoard that shocked the world," BBC (www.bbc.com)

Rancho Obi-Wan (ranchoobiwan.org)

"The Cullinan Diamond," Royal Collection Trust (www.rct.uk)

"Windsor Castle," Royal Collection Trust (www.rct.uk)

Seshan, K. S. S. "The story of a Hyderabad Nizam and his diamond paper weight," *The Hindu* (www.thehindu.com)

"Species profiles," Rainforest Alliance (www.rainforest-alliance.org)

"1637 Tulipmania," Rijksmuseum (www.rijksmuseum.nl)

Roberts, D. "Secrets of the Maya: Deciphering Tikal," *Smithsonian Magazine* (www.smithsonianmag.com)

"William Shakespeare Biography," Shakespeare Birthplace Trust (www.shakespeare.org)

Sir John Soane's Museum, London (www.soane.org)

Smithsonian (www.si.edu)

"Discover Ancient Rock Art in Australia's Northern Territory," *Smithsonian Magazine* (www.smithsonianmag.com)

"Rarities," Smithsonian National Postal Museum (postalmuseum.si.edu)

The State Hermitage Museum (www.hermitagemuseum.org)

Stonard, J.-P. "Hokusai: the Great Wave that swept the world," *The Guardian* (www.theguardian.com)

Switek, B. "Earliest known dino relative found," *Nature* (www.nature.com)

Tébar, M. "Spain's hard-won shipwreck coins finally go on public display in Cartagena," *El País* (elpais.com)

Trachtman, P. "The Secrets of Easter Island," *Smithsonian Magazine* (www.smithsonianmag.com)

"The Book of Kells," Trinity College Dublin (www.tcd.ie)

"In Pictures: Holy Relics of Prophet Mohammed exhibited in Topkapi Palace," *TRTWorld* (www.trtworld.com)

"Magna Carta," UK Parliament (www.parliament.uk)

Uluru-Kata Tjuta National Park (parksaustralia.gov.au/uluru)

UNESCO (whc.unesco.org)

"Fort Knox Bullion Depository," Unite States Mint (www.usmint.gov)

"Mammoth Cave: Explore the World's Longest Cave," U.S. Department of the Interior (www.doi.gov)

"Itsukushima Shrine," Visit Hiroshima (visithiroshima.net)

Vatican Library (www.vaticanlibrary.va)

"Sistine Chapel," Vatican Museums (www.museivaticani.va)

Whydah Pirate Museum (www.discoverpirates.com)

Wilkinson, E. *Chinese History: A Manual* (2000, Cambridge, MA: Harvard University Press)

"Rai of Yap — The Stone Money," *Wondermondo* (www.wondermondo.com)

World Wide Fund for Nature (www.worldwildlife.org)

Zimmer, K. "Why the Amazon doesn't really produce 20% of the world's oxygen," *National Geographic* (www.nationalgeographic.co.uk)

What on Earth Books is an imprint of What on Earth Publishing
The Black Barn, Wickhurst Farm, Tonbridge, Kent TN11 8PS, United Kingdom
30 Ridge Road Unit B, Greenbelt, Maryland, 20770, United States

First published in the United States in 2021

Written by David Long
Illustrated by Studio Muti

Staff for this book: Editor, Patrick Skipworth; Art Director, Andy Forshaw;
Designer, Daisy Symes

Library of Congress Cataloging-in-Publication Data available upon request

ISBN: 978-1-9129205-0-1

Printed in Malaysia

10 9 8 7 6 5 4 3 2 1

MIX
Paper from
responsible sources
FSC® C012700

whatonearthbooks.com